'Life is a combination of magic and pasta'
(Federico Fellini, Italian filmmaker)

Editing: Desirée Verkaar

Final editing: Elles van Genugten

Coordination: Claire Eversdijk

Art direction & design: Myrthe Bergboer, Suzanne Groenewegen

Photography: Food4Eyes.com, Claire Eversdijk, Freek Stoltenborgh, Remco Lassche

Styling: Lize Boer

Assistant publisher: Josje Kets

Publisher Pieter Harts

Food & recipes: Stefano Manti, Thea Spierings

English translation: Trahern Gemmell for Textcase, Hilversum, Netherlands

With thanks to:

David Mulder, Dille & Kamille, Lifestyle,

Tafel & Meer, Zus & Zo Keukengerei

This book was developed in close cooperation with Grand'Italia.

© Visconti, 2007

© English edition: Miller Books

email: info@miller-books.com

www.miller-books.com

1st printing 2007

2nd printing 2008

978 90 8724 051 6

Everything You Need To
Know About

Pasta

Contents

Introduction	13
Golden rules	19
Dried Pasta	20
Long pasta (pasta lunga)	26
Short pasta (pasta corta)	28
Filled pasta and pasta for stuffing	30
Soup pasta or pastine	30
Tomato sauce	32
Fresh Pasta	34
Base	36
Step-by-step	37
Basic pasta dough recipe	37
Making ravioli	38
Making tortellini	39
Cutting tagliatelle by hand	40
Gnocchi	44
Cooking & serving pasta	49
Al dente to perfection	51
Kitchen tools	56
Classics	66
Tagliatelle alla Bolognese	68
Penne alla carbonara	70
Spaghetti alla Napoletana	72
Bucatini con le sarde	74
Farfalle alla boscaiola	78
Pappardelle alla lepre	80
Trenette alla Genovese	82
Spaghetti alle vongole	84
Gnocchi alla Romana	88
Ravioli di magro	90

(V) This symbol can be found alongside recipes containing no meat and/or fish.

(4) All recipes make four servings.

Lasagne al forno	92
Bucatini all'Amatriciana	94
Spaghetti con aglio e olio	98
Fettuccine all'Alfredo	100
Minestrone	102
Spaghetti alla puttanesca	106
Spaghetti alla marinara	108

Soups with Pasta 112

Spinach soup with mini noodles	114
Beef bouillon with spaghettini and meatballs	114
Fresh tomato soup with orecchiette	116
Bouillon with green peas and pancetta	118
Vegetable soup with tortellini	118
Tortellini in brodo rosso	120
Seafood bouillon with alfabetini	124
Minestrone with porcini mushrooms and chicken filets	124
Cabbage soup with pesto	126
Roasted vegetable soup with pipe rigate	128
Chicken soup with capelli d'angelo	128
Mushroom soup with conchiglie rigate	130

Pasta with vegetables and fresh herbs 134

Lasagnette with pomodorini and garlic	136
Tagliatelle with parsley-lemon oil	136
Fusilli tricolore with zucchini flowers	138
Spaghetti with olives, tomatoes and rocket	140
Spaghetti with fresh tomato sauce	140
Tagliatelle with artichoke hearts and capers	142
Mushroom lasagne	146
Pappardelle with sun-dried tomatoes and pine nuts	148
Perciatelli with spicy tomato sauce	148
Paglia e fieno with red pesto	150
Farfalle with green sauce	152
Macaroni with aubergine and mozzarella	152
Tagliatelle with spring vegetables	154

Pasta with meat and poultry 158

Green tagliatelle with chicken filets in white wine sauce	160
Pipe rigate with stewed beef and San Daniele	162
Tagliatelle with tenderloin and truffle sauce	162

Tortelloni prosciutto crudo in creamy tomato sauce 164

Malfadine with salame cacciatore 166

Maccheroncine with chicken filets in mushroom sauce 166

Whole-grain penne with sausage and roasted garlic 170

Fettuccelle with pork tenderloin in creamy mushroom sauce 172

Fusilli with minced lamb and mustard 174

Linguine with salami 176

Pipe rigate with parma ham and green peas 176

Pasta with fish & seafood 180

Linguine with scampi in garlic mustard sauce 182

Tortiglioni with spinach and olive tapenade 184

Tagliatelle with seabass and samphire 184

Cravattine with coquilles Saint Jacques 186

Fazzoletti with crab in cream sauce 188

Penne with fresh tuna and peppers 192

Conchiglie all'uovo with shrimp in creamy dill sauce 192

Penne rigate with anchovies and broccoli 194

Lasagnette with salmon and crème fraîche-chive sauce 196

Fusilli with fresh salmon, watercress and horseradish 196

Spaghetti with bottarga 200

Crisp-fried spaghetti with anchovies and breadcrumbs 202

Pasta with cheese & cream 206

Stringhetti with saffron 208

Three-cheese lasagne 210

Lasagne with mozzarella and béchamel 210

Pappardelle with asparagus carbonara 212

Tortiglioni with tomato and parmesan 216

Tagliatelle all'uovo with gorgonzola and sage 216

Ricotta gnocchi 218

Maccheroncini with pancetta and mascarpone 222

Pipe rigate with walnut pecorino sauce 222

Whole-grain spaghetti with roasted peppers and goat's cheese 224

Penne with pear, pistachio and gorgonzola 228

Pipe rigate with ricotta nut sauce 228

Fettuccine with spinach and fontina 230

Pasta salads 234

Penne with aged cheese and avocado 236

Mezzi rigatoni with snow peas and tuna 236

Fusilli bucati with bresaola and rocket   238

Black linguine with pulpo salad   242

Gnocchi salad with fresh crab and rocket   244

Mezzi rigatoni with chicken and white asparagus   244

Fusilli with salmon and seafood   246

Penne salad with tuna tapenade   248

Orecchiette with beans and raisins   248

Filled Pasta   254

Caramella with smoked salmon and lemon cream sauce   256

Tortellini with veal and parmesan   256

Ravioli with peppers, ricotta, aubergine and mascarpone   258

Ravioli with artichoke mousse and tomato sauce   262

Tortellini ricotta e spinaci with mushroom sauce   264

Tortellini tricolore with sweet pepper sauce   264

Conchiglioni with ricotta, green peas and béchamel   266

Canneloni with purslane, ricotta and tomato sauce   270

Tortellini formaggio   272

Open lasagne with tomato, pesto and goat's cheese   274

Canneloni with spinach and aged cheese   274

Ravioli with hazelnut mascarpone sauce   276

Index   282

Seasonings – Olive oil   96

Seasonings – Pesto alla Genovese   110

Seasonings – Fresh herbs   132

Seasonings – Italian meats and dried sausage   156

Seasonings – Preserved anchovies   178

Seasonings – Italian cheeses   204

Seasonings – Garlic   214

Seasonings – Italian tomatoes   220

Seasonings – Balsamic vinegar   232

Seasonings – Olives & capers   252

Seasonings – Chilli peppers & spices   278

Contrary to popular belief, pasta does absolutely not make you fat. A normal portion of boiled pasta contains roughly three hundred calories and a lot of vitamins, minerals and proteins – especially if it's egg pasta. And even rich and creamy pasta dishes such as Alfredo (cream and cheese) and carbonara (with ham and egg yolks) are comparatively easy on your figure. Pasta's dubious reputation for weight gain comes from people putting far too much sauce on their pasta. The Italians are much more reserved on this count: the pasta and the sauce must maintain a certain balance without one overwhelming the other. Of course, good quality pasta is perfectly nutricious and delicious all on its own!

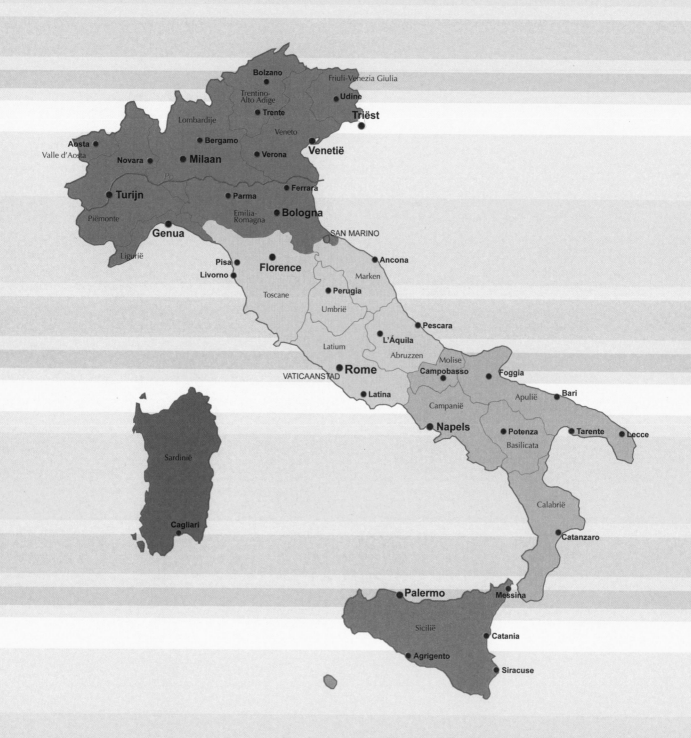

Bolzano

Trentino-
Alto Adige

Friuli-Venezia Giulia

Udine

Trente

Triëst

Lombardije

Veneto

Bergamo

Verona

Venetië

Aosta

Valle d'Aosta

Milaan

Novara

Po

Ferrara

Turijn

Parma

Bologna

Piëmonte

Emilia-
Romagna

Genua

SAN MARINO

Ligurië

Pisa

Ancona

Florence

Marken

Livorno

Toscane

Perugia

Umbrië

Pescara

Latium

L'Áquila

Abruzzen

Molise

Rome

Campobasso

Foggia

VATICAANSTAD

Latina

Apulië

Bari

Sardinië

Campanië

Napels

Potenza

Tarente

Lecce

Basilicata

Cagliari

Calabrië

Catanzaro

Palermo

Messina

Sicilië

Catania

Agrigento

Siracuse

Introduction

Italians and Pasta

If there is one thing that symbolises Italian cuisine, it's pasta. For many Italians, a meal is not complete without it. The average Italian eats around twenty-five kilos of pasta each year. In the north, a good deal of rice (risotto) is also eaten, but in the southern part of the country there's pasta on the table at least once a day, and sometimes twice. At lunch it's pastasciutta (pasta with sauce), for dinner pasta in brodo (in bouillon) or minestra (thick soup with pasta). It's no wonder southern Italians well exceed the annual twenty-five-kilo national average.

Eternal Pasta

Italian pasta has a fascinating history which goes back for literally hundreds of years. The country and its national culinary pride seem eternally inseparable. Illustrations going back almost two and a half thousand years, were discovered in an Etruscan tomb depicting a kind of early pasta machine: one implement for rolling out the dough and another, a sort of toothed wheel, most likely used for making spaghetti – and perhaps even a type of primitive – ravioli. A famous first-century Roman writer, Apicius, reports something similar: a dough that was made into small sheets, filled, then roasted. Pasta appeared in Sicily five centuries later. It was probably here that the dough was first boiled in water rather than baked or roasted. The word 'maccheroni' appears to hail from this island as well. 'Maccaruni' is Sicilian for 'formed into dough by force'. The Middle Ages gave us diverse recipes, descriptions and other indications that pasta was becoming more and more important as a basic foodstuff throughout most of the country. Even then, there were already clear regional differences in shape and manner of preparation. In the seventeenth century, the Neapolitans developed dried pasta, an invention which made it easier and more efficient to produce, taking it from the bread board to the factory. Naples remained an important bulwark of pasta manufacture. Consequently, this foodstuff slowly but surely conquered the entire world, partly with the help of Italian immigrants in America and Great Britain.

From region to region…

Italy as a nation did not exist before 1861. It was in this year that the diverse collection of independent regions and city-states like Venice, Genoa and Milan finally unified into a single country. Perhaps nowhere are these regional histories more evident than in their cuisines. It is rather a misnomer to talk about 'Italian food'. Each region has its own typical dishes and unique culinary traditions. One village will tell you that a certain pasta sauce just isn't complete without a good splash of red wine while another further on will swear that not a drop of wine should go into this sauce. This might have as much to do with the Italian character as regional differences. In any case, where food is concerned, many Italians stick to the quality and traditions they know – you will often hear it said that no cooking is better than that of your own mama or grandmother. This applies just as much to pasta as to anything else. It's true that pasta has conquered the entire country, starting

with the south, but as far as the form and the sauce that goes on it, Italy is just as diverse as it was before 1861.

As a generalisation, you can say that the south of Italy, where the sauces are made with an olive oil base, prefers its noodles thin, fine and long. Many southern dishes are classically light and simple, such as spaghetti alla Napoletana, an elementary sauce of tomato, olive oil and fresh basil. In the cooler northern regions you will find more butter and cream in the sauces, making for a perfect combination with the shorter, more substantial fresh egg noodle varieties: fresh ravioli or tortellini with ricotta and white sauce, for example, or pasta boscaiole from the area around Milan, served with a rich mushroom cream sauce.

365 x Pasta

True pasta lovers have known for a long time, that you can eat it every day of the year without ever having the same thing on your plate twice. There are literally hundreds of pasta varieties. There are the long kinds (pasta lunga) such as vermicelli and spaghetti, long flat kinds such as (from narrow to broad) trenette, fettuccine, tagliatelle and pappardelle, and hollow kinds like maccheroni. Then there are the short varieties (pasta corta) such as penne (quills), fusilli (spirals) and farfalle (bowties – or butterflies, if you prefer) and the filled kinds like ravioli and tortellini. There are pastas coloured with spinach, tomato, saffron, beets and even octopus ink; pastas flavoured with garlic, chillis, truffle or, yes, chocolate.

What do you mean, al dente?

Many people think cooking pasta is more complicated than it really is. These days, everyone insists that pasta must be al dente, (literally 'on the tooth') meaning still firm inside. It's true, of course – the last thing you want is to end up with overcooked pasta in a watery sauce. You also don't want to end up with pasta, which is still hard inside and tastes like uncooked flour. There was a time when pasta was often cooked much too long. But the trend now seems to be shifting to the other extreme.

You will find a step-for-step guide in the chapter on cooking and serving pasta, a little aid to help you put perfect noodles on the table, time and again.

Golden Rules

✓ Always go for top-quality dried Italian pasta or make your own from scratch.

✓ Cook pasta in a large pot with a lot of boiling water.

✓ Don't forget to put plenty of salt in the water.

✓ Keep an eye on the pasta as it cooks and fish out a piece of pasta to test if it's ready.

✓ Strain the pasta the moment it's ready (don't rinse it!), and do not drain it completely.

✓ Choose natural, flavourful ingredients. Sun-ripened tomatoes and good-quality olive oil make a world of difference.

✓ Each pasta variety has its own perfect companion. Short, hollow pasta cries out for thick, chunky sauces. The thinner the pasta, the lighter the sauce.

✓ Be careful not to overwhelm the pasta with too much sauce.

✓ There is an Italian saying: 'pasta does not wait for people, people wait for pasta'. That means you should dig in as soon as your plate's in front of you!

Pasta secca... shells, snails, bow ties, angel hair... anyone who looks beyond the 'normal' pasta varieties will discover the most enchanting and inventive shapes. Italians distinguish between two general types: short pasta *(pasta corta)* such as penne, farfalle and fusilli, and long pasta *(pasta lunga)* such as spaghetti and tagliatelle. There are also ready-made filled types of pasta in dried form, such as tortel lini and ravioli, and shapes you can fill on your own, such as the large, hollow, pipe-like canneloni or those large shells called conchigli.

Each of these 'categories', of course, contains literally hundreds of varieties. Not only does each region have its own traditional pastas but commercial producers are also constantly developing new forms. It is said that new pasta

Dried Pasta

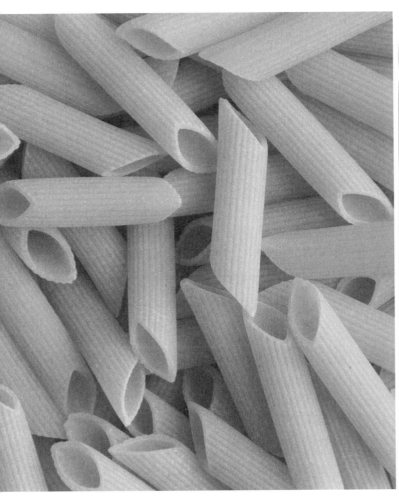 

varieties appear on the market as often as new models on the Milan catwalk! To make things even trickier, there are different names for the same shape in different places. Tagliatelle is called 'fettuccine' in Rome and Italian maccheroni is generally not the elbow pasta we know as macaroni but long, hollow tubes. Maccheroni appears in different lengths, and in some regions the name refers to pasta in general.

So, don't despair if you can't find the type of pasta your recipe calls for – there is a wealth of possibilities and no hard and fast rules. Above all, consider which pasta is best suited to the sauce you have in mind. Foremost, it must be able to hold the sauce and other ingredients. You will have the best luck if you combine short, hollow shapes with thick, chunky sauces and long, thin pasta with thin, smooth sauces.

The first pasta machines

The city of Naples was home to the first true pasta factory. At the beginning of the nineteenth century, Neapolitans were making and drying pasta on quite a large scale, much of it for export. Factory workers kneaded the dough with the same tool used by winemakers – their feet. Ferdinand II, then King of Naples, put an end to this when he hired an engineer to invent a device which could do the same thing. From that point on, dough was kneaded and cut by machine. Naples remained the centre of pasta production, not least of all due to its climate, which is ideal for air-drying pasta. Humid weather would make the pasta mouldy and overly dry weather quickly turned the dough crumbly. The use of machines made it possible to export more and more dried pasta. A lot of it was shipped to America, where thousands of Italian immigrants craved their native dishes.

During the course of the nineteenth century, better machines were developed to sift the flour, knead the dough and press it into the proper shapes. New technology meant that the holes through which the pasta was pressed could be formed with ever greater precision. This enabled the creation of a vast array of new and beautiful shapes that could not be made at home. The various factories continued releasing new varieties in the hope that they would become a hit. By the end of the nineteenth century there were already hundreds of different pasta shapes. Ultimately, it was the most 'functional' designs which became most popular, such as fusilli, which is perfect for holding sauce due to its spiral shape.

Singing pasta

Making perfect al dente pasta requires patient care and attention. It's best for beginners to test the noodles now and again to see how they're doing. But not for an Italian cook, no sir. They have so much experience that they can actually hear whether the pasta boiling in the pot is al dente. The noodles, they say, start singing.

Quality pasta

You can buy dried pasta in a thousand and one different varieties and at vastly divergent prices. It is really not necessary to always buy the most expensive and exclusive brands available. One difference, however, is that the cheaper varieties are often made with soft wheat flour or a mix of hard and soft. This kind of pasta is less firm and will quickly become soft and sticky after cooking. When buying pasta, pay attention to whether this is made from one hundred percent durum (hard) flour: *pasta di semola di grano duro*, in proper Italian. Or, in the case of egg pasta: grano duro e uova. When buying coloured pasta, it's important to make sure there are no artificial colouring agents. The Grand'Italia brand is a good choice for quality Italian pasta.

The best factory pasta

The best Italian dried factory pasta is produced using bronze plates through which the dough is pressed into the desired shape. The bronze lends the noodles (anything from spaghetti to fusilli) a more raw surface texture than steel or teflon can provide. The difference is hardly visible but you will notice that the sauce sticks better to bronze-pressed pasta because of its special texture.

Factory pasta

Pasta machines have become increasingly sophisticated over time. Today, the entire production process – from mixing, kneading, shaping and drying to packaging – is automated. Two separate 'dosers' maintain just the right proportion of flour to water. These are the only two ingredients in most factory pasta, though some recipes call for other additions, such as vegetables, saffron or octopus ink to create the proper colour or flavour. Good pasta contains no artificial colourings, flavourings or other additives. Egg pasta can also be factory-made. Usually the egg is mixed into the dough in a powder form, though fresh eggs are used in some cases. The liquid must be evenly absorbed by the flour for the dough to reach a homogeneous consistency. First, the ingredients go into the mixer. The resulting dough is then kneaded for ten to twenty minutes in a kneading machine. The dough is not rolled out and cut, as it is when made at home, but pushed through a press by a revolving screw. The apertured heads that give the pasta its desired shape are perhaps the most important component of this machine, because the noodles must be perfectly formed. If the product is not the same thickness throughout it will never cook evenly. After this, a revolving blade cuts the pasta into the correct length. Long pasta falls right out of the press onto a horizontal stave whereas short pasta is spread out on a conveyor belt. The noodles are then exposed to hot air in two different drying chambers. Once dry, the noodles are finally weighed, packaged and shipped off to the stores.

Pasta Lunga Spaghetti Chitarra d'angelo Tagliatelle Bavette **Mafalde** Pappardelle Lasagne Maccheroni Ziti Rigatoni Mafaldine Fusilli Tortellini **Casoncelli** Tagliatelle Radiatori Rigati **Rigatoni** stortini Spaghettini conchigliettes

Linguine **Vermicelli** Fedelini Capelli
Frappe Fettuccine Trenette
Bucatini Gnocchi Napoletani **Mezzi**
Capellini **Agnolotti** Ravioli **Panzarotti**
Tagliolini Orecchiette penette
Tortelloni ditali Gramigna
Cravattine fieno fusilli

Long pasta *(pasta lunga)*

Round spaghetti, square chitarra, flat tagliatelle, oval linguine, hollow bucatini... Long pastas aren't all just strands of the same; they come in all sorts, shapes and sizes. The finest, 'angel hair', is only one millimetre thick and goes well with light sauces and clear bouillons. Broad pappardelle, on the other hand, are more than two centimetres wide and are excellent with a chunky ragù and stewed game, such as *pappardelle con le lepre* (pappardelle and rabbit), a Tuscan favourite. And between these two extremes lies a world of possibilities.

Capelli d'angelo

These long, fine threads have been beautifully christened 'capelli d'angelo', or 'angel hair', after their delicate, thin shape. They are also simply called capellini, or 'little hairs'. This is the very thinnest of the long pasta varieties, only around one millimetre in width. They are usually twisted into nests before being dried. This prevents the fragile strands from breaking during packaging and transport. Fine, smooth sauces go well with capellini. They are often broken into smaller pieces before being mixed into soups. They are also commercially available in this form (short strands), illustrated below.

Maccheroni, ziti and bucatini

In Italy, the word 'maccheroni' is often used as a general term for all pasta. It specifically refers to long, tubular noodles of various lengths and thicknesses. The pasta's hollow shape makes it great for holding sauce. Bucatini are also hollow strands (buco means 'hole' or 'pit') but thinner, with a diameter of around two-and-a-half millimetres. Bucatini originally come from Sicily, where they are served with a sauce of fresh sardines. Ziti is thicker than maccheroni and is often broken into pieces before boiling.

Mafaldine and lasagnette

Mafalde and mafaldine are long, flat noodles with two wavy edges. Mafalde are about ten millimetres wide, mafaldine somewhat less. They are also referred to as tagliatelle nervate. Their undulating ridges look quite pretty on the plate, though this is not their primary function. The edges are cusped in this manner to help keep the sauce on the pasta. Broader ribbon pastas, such as lasagne and pappardelle, and more narrow varieties like trenette en lasagnette, have sometimes one, sometimes two such edges.

Pappardelle and lasagne

Pappardelle is a long, broad ribbon pasta about two centimetres wide, sometimes with one or two wavy edges. It enjoys great popularity in Umbria and Tuscany. Lasagne is broader yet (sometimes even square) and is usually used for casserole dishes *like the well-known lasagne al forno ('baked lasagne') which consists of layered noodles, sauce and cheese,* or cannelloni, which is made by rolling pre-cooked noodles into cylinders which are then stuffed with some kind of filling. Normal lasagne is often pre-boiled, though this is not always necessary. Raw noodles may be used if the sauce is thinner than usual, as they will absorb a lot of liquid when baking.

Spaghetti, chitarra and linguine

The most famous of them all is spaghetti, which literally means 'little strings'. Usually these strands are around thirty centimetres in length, though there are longer varieties. The thickness varies as well, with two millimetres being the average. Extra-thin spaghetti is called 'spaghettini' and extra-thick, 'spaghettoni'. Basillicata is one area where the traditional spaghetti alla chitarra is still made. The dough for this pasta is pressed through a stringed tool aptly called a chitarra ('guitar') with a rolling pin. This creates strands which are square rather than circular. Linguine (literally 'little tongues') are long, oval strands.

Stringozzi and stringhetti

Stringozzi is an Umbrian ribbon pasta which is somewhat thicker and firmer than spaghetti and has an ovaline, rather than round, diameter. This gives it a somewhat chewier texture. Stringhetti is a relatively recent invention and falls somewhere between stringozzi and spaghetti.

Vermicelli and fedelini

Vermicelli, like spaghetti, are long circular strands. The name means 'little worms'. In the south of Italy the word 'vermicelli' is often used as a synonym for spaghetti, though it usually refers to a somewhat thinner variety. Vermicelli is not only delicious in soup but can be served with different kinds of smooth (especially cream) sauces – which is the custom in Naples – or with tomato sauce and Venus clams. As with spaghetti, vermicelli comes in different thicknesses. There are vermicelloni (extra thick) and vermicellini (extra thin). Fedelini is a comparable pasta variety, which is sometimes even thinner than vermicelli.

Tagliatelle and bavette

Tagliare is the Italian verb 'to cut' and many Italian cooks still make their own tagliatelle by rolling up sheets of pasta dough and cutting them into ribbons. Tagliarelli is synonymous with tagliatelle, though it often refers to a narrower variety. Tagliarellini, taglierini, tagliatelline and tagliolini are also thinner pastas. They vary in width and thickness depending on the producer. Tagliatelle are usually eight to ten millimetres wide and 0.8 millimetres thick, while the miniature varieties are considerably narrower, around three millimetres. In the south of Italy tagliatelle is sometimes called 'bavette', though this is actually a thinner variety.

Fettuccine and trenette

Fettuccine, or fettucce, are long, flat ribbons. They are generally just a little narrower than tagliatelle, six to eight millimetres. 'Fettucelle' and 'fettucce romana' usually refer to normal tagliatelle. Ligurian trenette are slightly narrower, about three millimetres in width. This pasta is traditionally served up as trenette alla Genovese with basil pesto, potatoes and haricots verts.

Paglia e fieno

The name of this decorative ribbon pasta means 'hay and straw'. It comes in various widths and is often sold as bicolore. They are used the same way as normal tagliatelle, though often served in ways which highlight their contrasting colours.

Short pasta (pasta corta)

The world of short pastas is even more eclectic than that of the long varieties. By the end of the nineteenth century, pasta machines had become so advanced that it was possible to press dough into all sorts of fantastic shapes, limited only by the imagination of the manufacturers. There are hundreds of shapes and new ones are constantly being released. The most important thing is for the sauce to find its 'niche' in the noodles. Take orecchiette, for example; these are basically miniature bowls for holding sauce. Some varieties are splendidly designed in all manner of shapes, including little hearts, making it food for the eyes and the belly!

Gnocchetti

These little ribbed bowls look a bit like a hollow version of gnocchi, the boiled or baked dumplings made with a mix of flour and potato. To make things even more confusing, there is a larger version of gnocchetti, also called gnocchi. This is not the same as the famous gnocchi di patate or gnocchi alla romana.

Gramigna

Gramigna are hollow, curved noodles, a specialty which hails from Emilia-Romagna. Another short, somewhat thinner noodle such as pennette or sedanini can be substituted for gramigna if necessary.

Rigatoni

This tube pasta has a larger diameter than penne and straight-cut ends where penne has slants. The name simply means 'ribbed' or 'ridged', referring to the noodles' linear grooves. Mezzi rigatoni means 'half rigatoni', the noodles being half as long.

Pipe

These short, thick, curved little tubes somewhat resemble a compacted version of the famous 'elbow macaroni'. Pipe hold their sauce exceedingly well, even chunkier sauces with pieces of meat or vegetables. They often have ridges, referred to then as pipe rigate.

Penne

Penne is the Italian word for quill and comes from a time when goose feathers were used for writing. These diagonally cut hollow tubes are indeed reminiscent of an old-fashioned pen. Penne come in many sizes – thin pennine, mezze penne ('half penne') which are cut in half lengthwise, and extra-large pennoni are just a few. Penne rigate are like normal penne but with ridges.

Tortiglioni

Tortiglioni (or *torciglioni*) look like penne rigate but are a little thicker and have ridges which spiral across the surface of the noodles where penne rigate has straight lines. They are equally tasty in the same dishes, especially with thick, hearty sauces.

Lumache and conchiglie

Lumache and conchiglie, or 'snails' and 'shells', are both quite popular due to their ideal shapes. Both are available in extra-large versions, which are often stuffed then baked in the oven, called lumaconi and conchiglioni, respectively.

Farfalle

Farfalle, which means both 'butterflies' and 'bowties', is one of the most popular pastas in Italy. Strichetti is another word for this variety. The kind with round 'wings' are called farfalle ronde. They go well with a wide array of sauces and are also excellent in pasta salad.

Orecchiette

These tiny bowl-like 'little ears' from Puglia are perfect for holding sauce. They are still sometimes made by hand – miniature sheets of dough pressed with the thumb to form pits. They are traditionally eaten with a sauce of broccoli and anchovies.

Fusilli and eliche

Fusilli are short, spiral-shaped noodles. They used to be made by hand by winding a strand of dough around a thin stick. *Eliche means* 'screws', an appropriate moniker given their unique shape. Eliche are often sold as fusilli. Though the two types are similar, when placed side by side there is a clear distinction: fusilli are more open, eliche more compact.

Rotelline and ruote

These 'little wagon wheels' stay nice and firm during the boiling process, making them well-suited for eating with thick, hearty sauces. They hold their shapes quite well in salads too. They are often sold as tricolore, that is in three colours: red, green and white (tomato, spinach and plain) like the Italian flag. Ruote are the larger version of rotelline.

Lasagnette and festonelle

Lasagnette refers both to full-length, narrower lasagna noodles, often with wavy edges, as well as to narrower noodles cut into shorter pieces. They are also called festonelle or, if cut into diagonal pieces, pantacce.

Filled pasta and pasta for stuffing

Ravioli and tortellini can be bought dried and with various fillings. They usually contain cheese and beef or pork mixed with bread crumbs and herbs. In Italy, these dried filled pastas usually go into soups. *Tortellini in brodo* is a popular dish of filled pasta rings in a clear (usually beef) bouillon. There are also dried pastas that you can fill with whatever you want. Ready-made cannelloni (the word means 'big pipes/reeds') are often easier to use than lasagna noodles, which must be folded around the filling. In Calabria they are stuffed with a mixture of spicy beef and pecorino cheese, though of course anything is possible. Conchiglioni and lumaconi, large pasta 'shells' and 'snail's shells' are also designed for filling. They are usually stuffed, then baked.

Soup pasta (pastine)

There are miniature pastas especially designed for soup, *called pastine*. *Alfabetini* ('little letters'), *risoni* (pasta shaped like grains of rice), semi di melone ('melon seeds'), stelline ('little stars'), farfalline ('little butterflies' or 'little bow-ties') and conchigliette ('little shells') are all delicious in broth (in brodo) as well as in vegetable soups like minestrone. Illustrated below: saporini sardi, maccarroneddos and tubettini.

Colours

Many pasta varieties also come in a green version (verdi) which is coloured with spinach. Octopus ink is used to achieve the unusual hue of black pasta (nero). Tricolore pasta usually consists of plain pasta, green pasta with spinach and reddish orange pasta with tomato. Beet juice turns pasta a deep magenta. Other ingredients used to give pasta special colours and flavours are paprika, pumpkin, saffron, corn, nettle, red and black pepper... the list goes on and on. Whole-grain pasta (integrali) is a bit darker than the normal variety. If you look carefully you can see the fibres in the pasta, and feel them on your tongue – the consistency is much coarser than that of white pasta.

Tomato sauce
Sugo di pomodoro (makes four servings)

400g (14oz) tomatoes (fresh or peeled Italian tomatoes in the tin)

2 tbsp olive oil

1 carrot, finely chopped

1 onion, minced

1 celery stalk, finely chopped

2 cloves of garlic, pressed

1 red chilli pepper, seeded and minced

2 tbsp fresh herbs (basil, parsley, oregano, thyme)

salt and pepper

1 Peel and coarsely chop the fresh tomatoes. If using tinned tomatoes, cut them into large chunks and drain.

2 Heat the olive oil in a pan. Sauté the carrot, onion and celery until the onion is translucent, then add the garlic and chilli pepper.

3 Stir in the tomato and herbs.

4 Add salt and pepper to taste and allow the mixture to simmer, stirring occasionally, until it has cooked down to a thick sauce. If you want a smooth sugo, the sauce can be pushed through a sieve.

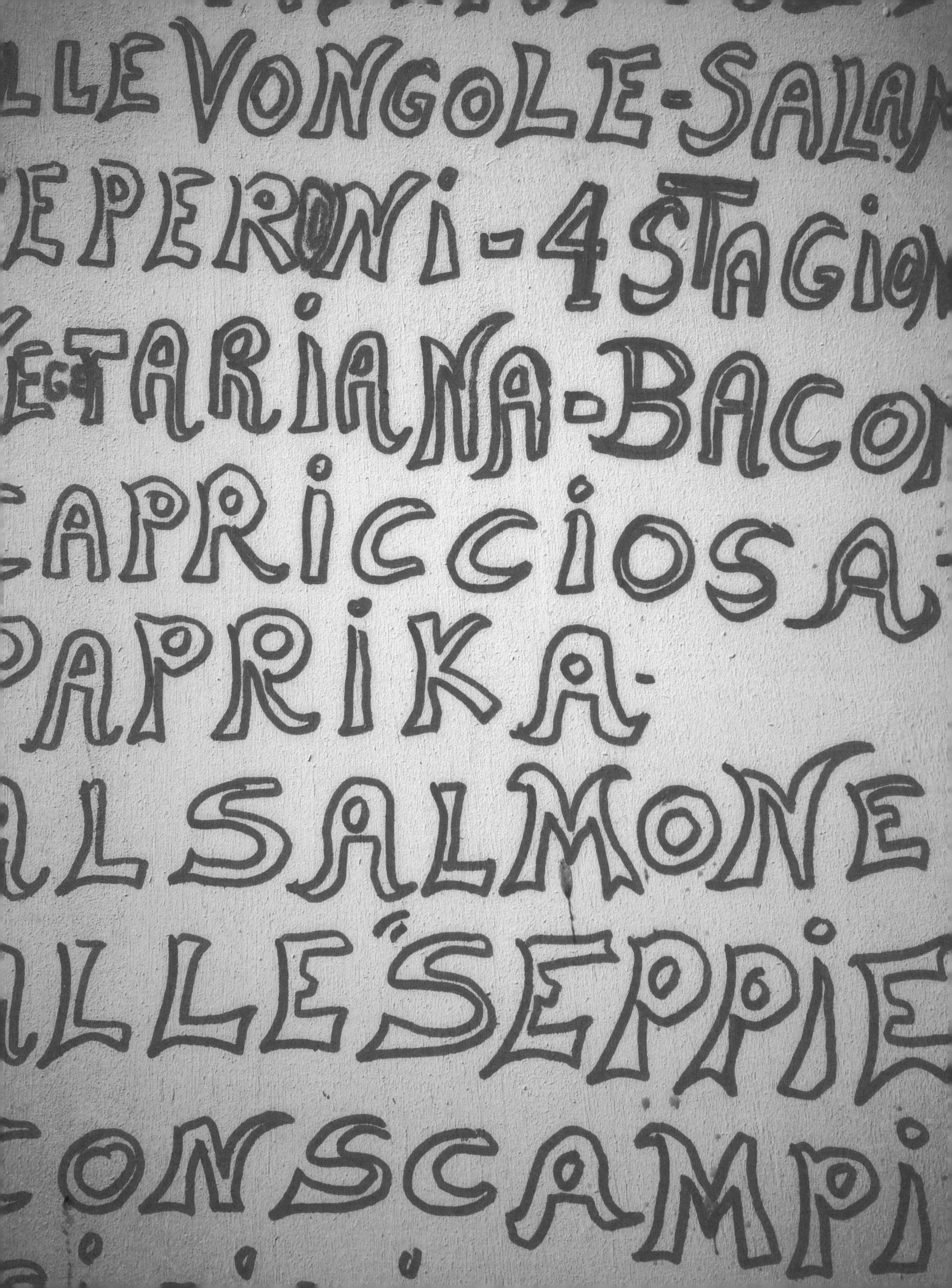

LLE VONGOLE · SALA

E PERONI · 4 STAGIO

EGETARIANA · BACO

CAPRICCIOSA ·

PAPRIKA ·

AL SALMONE

LLE SEPPIE

CON SCAMPI

There may well be nothing better than fresh, home-made pasta. Silky ribbons that capture and absorb the flavour of the sauce, so simple yet so evocative... Who are you going to indulge first; your family, your best friends – or are you going to keep it all for yourself? In northern and central Italy, people tend to prefer to make their own pasta from scratch. The pasta in these parts is rich and full-

Fresh pasta

flavoured because eggs usually go into the dough, and therefore go perfectly with white sauces of panna (cream) or butter which are traditional in the north. Soft fresh pasta absorbs some of the butter and holds the sauce, forming a delicious layer all around.

Making pasta at home is a whole lot easier than you might think, especially if you have a few tools such as a pasta machine (these are not at all difficult to use). And if you keep a supply of your own home-made dough in the freezer, you will have delicious, fresh pasta always ready to serve up. Even if there have been disappointments in the past, with the tips and step-by-step instructions in this chapter, you can't go wrong!

The base

Some think that making pasta at home is a difficult and strenuous task, nothing but wrestling with dough and getting covered in flour. Anyone who claims this most likely used the wrong type of flour. Fortunately, it's getting easier and easier to find good pasta semolina.

The grain

It is essential that the grain being used contains sufficient gluten. This is necessary for firmness and elasticity, ensuring that the dough can easily be rolled out without tearing. Hard, or durum, wheat (grano duro) contains the most gluten and is the best option. This variety has a hard, compact kernel – hence the name.

For fresh egg pasta you can also use Italian grano tenero flour. Grano tenero is a somewhat softer variety of wheat, containing less gluten, which results in softer pasta. But watch out: the literal translation of grano tenero is 'soft wheat', but this type is a good deal harder and more gluten-rich than the European soft wheat from which normal pastry flour is produced. Do not confuse the two, as pastry flour is really not suited to making pasta. All-purpose flour is a bit harder and can be used if combined with durum semolina. It's rare to see pasta made from other grains, with the exception of buckwheat pasta, which can be found in the Italian Alps.

Type 00

Different types of flour are made from these kernels, with tipo 00 (pronounced tipo doppio zero) being the finest and best-suited variety. This designation, though, refers only to the milling process and does not necessarily mean that the flour is suitable for pasta dough. There is also type 00 flour for making bread.

Eggs

Fresh pasta can be made using a small amount of water, though most home pasta-makers prefer egg. You can use egg yolks instead of whole eggs by substituting two yolks for each whole egg. This will make the dough richer in flavour and a deeper yellow.

Step-by-Step

Basic pasta dough recipe (makes four servings):

300g (10.5oz) Italian flour (*type 'OO'*)

3 eggs (or 150ml (5oz) water)

half tsp salt

Make a pile of the semolina on a clean, dry surface. Form a pit in the centre, into which you break the eggs or pour in the water. Using a fork, carefully stir from the middle outward until the semolina is well mixed with the egg or water. It's now time to knead. Knead the dough thoroughly for 10 to 15 minutes. This is necessary to activate the gluten.

1

If the dough is too moist, add a little more flour; if too dry, add a little water. You can tell whether you've kneaded long enough by the consistency; the dough should become more elastic, supple and softer in texture. Cover the dough in plastic wrap and let it sit for at least half an hour in a cool place. If you skip this step, the dough might become too elastic and difficult to work with.

2

Divide the ball of dough into smaller pieces if necessary. You will need about 75 grams per person. The leftover dough can be put in plastic wrap and frozen for future use. It will keep for several months this way. Roll out the dough to a thickness of less than one centimetre.

3

It can now be put through the pasta machine. Start with the thickest setting and fold the sheet of dough double each time before putting it through again. Slowly but surely you will see it getting softer and more velvety in consistency. Once you've got it to the right thickness with the pasta machine, you can turn it into whatever shape you want. Try ravioli or tagliatelle for practice.

4

Making ravioli

Home-made ravioli looks great and is not difficult to make, though it does take some time. They can be round, oval or (most commonly) square. Once you've got the hang of it, you will have enough ravioli for the whole family before you know it.

1 Gently roll the dough out to a thin sheet using a rolling pin or pasta machine. If necessary, cut away the sides to form a straight rectangle. Imagine a line running down the middle of the sheet and place small mounds of filling on one side of this line. Slightly moisten the dough around the filling using a brush.

2 Carefully fold the sheet of dough double, covering the mounds of filling. Keep it loose to prevent the mounds from being pressed flat. Press the edges together a little to get the filling positioned, being careful not to press it too tight — you still have to leave room for the air to escape.

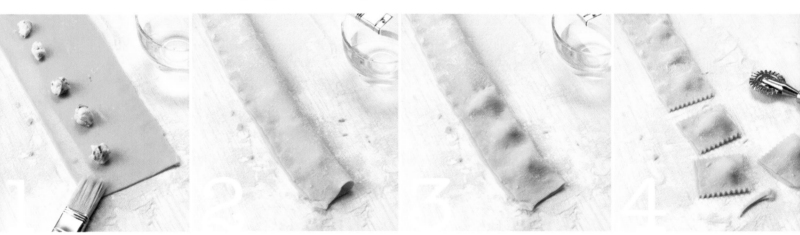

3 Gently press the dough closed around the filling with your fingers. Make sure that you get as much air out of the ravioli as possible, otherwise they might burst open during cooking. The parcels must be completely closed to prevent water from getting in and diluting the filling.

4 Once the parcels are ready, it's time to cut them apart. A specially designed dough wheel will give them lovely perforated edges, though this is not necessary. You can also make ridges in the edges using the prongs of a fork, or just leave them as they are. Keep between floured cloths.

Making tortellini

Legend has it that tortellini, the tasty little stuffed dough rings, were inspired by Venus' navel. The word 'tortellini' literally means 'tart-lets', which sounds almost as appealing!

Roll out a sheet of dough with a rolling pin or pasta machine. Cut small rounds out using a circular form. **1**

Place a small mound of filling on each round of dough and moisten the edges slightly with a brush. **2**

   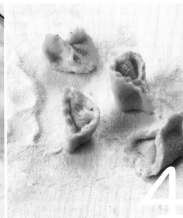

Fold each round double, making filled half-moons, and fold the ends in slightly. **3**

Now bring the ends together and press them until firmly closed. **4**

Hand-cut tagliatelle

You can make tagliatelle with the pasta machine, though cutting it by hand works just as well. The name is, after all, derived from the word 'tagliare', meaning 'to cut'. You can cut this pasta to any thickness, depending on the sauce and your own preference. Remember: if it's broader than two centimetres, it's no longer tagliatelle, but pappardelle.

1 Roll the dough out to an even layer and sprinkle a little flour over it to keep it from sticking later. If necessary, cut the sides down to form a nice clean rectangle.

2 Now roll the dough up endwise. Italian cooks have many different ways of doing this. Some fold the sheet double first, or several times even, or they fold the outermost edge around once so that they can afterwards toss the rolls open in one smooth serpentine motion. In reality, it makes little difference how you choose to roll it up.

3 Now slice the roll into small rings with a sharp knife. The knife should be sharp because you don't want to press down too hard as this will turn the roll into a single clump again. The knife should slide through as easily as possible. Wait to roll up the next sheet until the last has been cut, again to prevent the edges from sticking together. The longer you leave the dough rolled up, the higher the chance of this.

4 Unroll the rounds of dough and hang the resulting tagliatelle up over a horizontal stave or leave them spread out between two floured tea towels.

Italian specialty stores often sell refrigerated fresh pasta such as tagliatelle, fettuccine and pappardelle, and filled varieties like ravioli and tortellini. Even the larger supermarkets often have pre-packaged 'fresh' pasta. If you're pressed for time but have a craving for that fresh egg pasta, these are worth trying. Watch out for artificial colouring and flavouring agents, especially in the filled pastas. This often has a lot to say about the overall quality of the pasta.

In Italy, fresh pasta is divided into two types. In the south there's pasta fresca di grano duro (made with durum wheat and water), while the north has its characteristic fresca all'uovo, made with egg and the softer grano tenero flour.

Gnocchi

In Italy, gnocchi (pronounced 'nyockie') are almost always made fresh at home. They are delicious with butter and sage, drizzled with olive oil and covered with grated parmesan, soft gorgonzola, a fresh tomato sauce or a hearty meat ragù. Gnocchi are great for absorbing flavour due to their crinkled shape and soft texture.

Is this pasta or isn't it?

The word gnocchi translates roughly to 'lumps' or 'chunks', a name Italians give to just about all foods which are served in this form. Different parts of the country have different ideas about exactly what makes true gnocchi. This has given rise to some confusion about exactly how gnocchi is supposed to be made. The most famous variety is gnocchi de patate, made from potato puree mixed with a small amount of flour, kneaded into a dough and cut into small oval balls. As such, they are technically not a kind of pasta, due to the fact that the main ingredient is potato. The all-original gnocchi, though, did indeed consist of a dough made from flour and eggs which was cut into pieces and boiled or baked. *Gnocchi alla Romana* are still prepared in this manner. The addition of potato to the recipe came principally from the north of Italy, where someone in the eighteenth century realized this would be substantially cheaper to produce. The potato texture made them extra light and airy, an accidental smash success in many parts of the country.

Linguistic complications

You'll find that similar types of gnocchi are called different things in different parts of Italy, or the same name is used to refer to different types of gnocchi. The Italians themselves get confused, to say nothing of the rest of the world! Gnocchi from Genoa are called trofie. Here they are eaten with that world-famous local pesto sauce. In Florence, gnocchi are also called topini. (This, by the way, is the Italian word for 'mice' – a not very well informed American in the south of Italy once

Priest stranglers

In certain parts of Italy, gnocchi are also called strangolapreti or strozzapreti, meaning 'priest stranglers' or 'priest chokers'. The story goes that a priest once really did choke on a gnoccho.

caused an uproar in a restaurant, – by swearing that there were topini all over the place.) In some areas gnocchi are made from ricotta and spinach. In Lombardy these are called malfatti and in Tuscany – to really confuse you – ravioli, or sometimes *gnocchi del casentino*. There is also gnocchi *di zucca, made from pumpkin in place of potato. Ciciones* or *malloreddus are small Sicilian gnocchi, made from* flour coloured with saffron and served with a tomato and garlic-sausage sauce. And Trentino is known for all sorts of coloured gnocchi, such as the strozzapreti with spinach or red beetroot, served with a melted butter and poppy seed sauce or with gorgonzola.

'Gnocchi-fest'

There is a traditional festival in Verona called the bacanal *del gnoco*. The 'Father of the Gnocchi' (*Papà del Gnoco*) and the 'Duke of the Boiling Pot' (*Duca della Pignata*) take the lead in a carnivalesque procession of cheerfully dressed townspeople. Just before the period between Lent and Easter, these revellers enjoy one last meal of … yes, exactly.

It became official in 1577 in Genoa: pasta could only be produced with hard wheat flour from durum wheat. The local pasta makers' guild wrote this and many other regulations in 'Regolazione dell' Arte dei Maestri Fidelari' (guidelines of the pasta makers' guild).

Cooking & serving pasta

Italians speak fondly of pasta, almost as if it were a loved one. They find its gratitude its most beautiful quality. You need only give it a little attention and it will do exactly what you want and your dish really cannot go wrong. The most important thing is that it is cooked perfectly until al dente – just tender. Granted, this is a subjective term. Some like their pasta a little more firm than others (and that goes even for true Italians!). This is also regionally influenced. Pasta is served firmer in the south of Italy than in the north, for example. It's always a good idea to stay near the pot while the pasta is boiling to make sure that it doesn't overcook. As soon as it is done, the pasta requires your full and undivided attention. It is at its most delicious straight from the pot.

Ready? Go!

Make sure the sauce is ready, the table set, and everyone gathered round

Boil the water

Boil one litre (4 cups) of water for every 100g (3.5oz) of pasta and salt generously

Cook the pasta

Keep the pasta at a low boil, uncovered, stir occasionally

Taste it

Taste it now and again to see if it's tender – cooked until al dente

Strain it

Strain the pasta right away and mix it into the sauce

Serve it

Hand out the bowls and don't wait a minute longer!

Al dente to perfection

Cooking pasta is often made more complicated than it really needs to be.
Follow this handy guide and you will always have perfect pasta.

In Italy, when the cook calls out 'I'm putting the pasta in the pot!' it means 'get ready, dinner is served!'. From the moment you start, **everything must be ready:** the table set and hungry friends and family gathered round, the plates warmed, the colander ready in the sink and the sauce waiting patiently for a ladle.

Bring a **good amount of water** to the boil in a large pot: one litre (4 cups) per hundred grams (3.5oz) of pasta. Pasta will expand in the water and needs some 'elbow room' to prevent clumping. Also, make sure that the water does not lose too much of its heat when the pasta is put in, as this can also make it stick. Do not salt the water until it is boiling. In still water, the salt will sink to the bottom of the pot and cause a chemical reaction with the metal. Putting oil in the water to prevent sticking is a futile enterprise – it will just stay on top of the water.

Put all the pasta in at the same time to ensure that it cooks evenly. If using long pasta, insert it vertically and let it stand until it has softened, then push under. Stir once, then cover the pot to bring the water to a boil again as quickly as possible. If you're worried about it boiling over, set the lid slightly askew to let some steam escape. Once the water is boiling again, uncover the pot. Reduce the heat, making sure that the water keeps a boil. Stir the pasta now and again. The boiling process does not take long. Even half a minute too long can be disastrous for flavour and texture, so **just keep an eye on it.**

We can't say it often enough: pasta needs to be al dente, meaning tender, but still quite firm. Fine, fresh pasta sometimes only requires 30 seconds to be al dente, while thick dry pasta takes longer – sometimes close to a quarter-hour. Pay attention to the instructions on the package but, above all, **try it out for yourself.**

If the pasta is ready, **strain it immediately.** Set a little of the cooking water aside. In Italy, this is added to the sauce if it gets too thick. Shake the colander back and forth well to make sure the water drains, especially with hollow pastas. Immediately **mix** the pasta into the sauce or, depending on the recipe, the sauce into the pasta.

There are two proper Italian ways to serve pasta – either in a large bowl which is passed around the table, or in individual bowls. Either way, this is the moment when everybody seems to get really quiet. Forget niceties for a moment and just dig in, because the pasta is **now at its tastiest!**

How much per person?

The amount of pasta suggested per person varies enormously. This is because some recipes assume that the pasta is being served as the primo piatto, or first course, while other recipes intend it as the main course. There is also a big difference between fresh and dried pasta. Dried pasta will expand a good deal when boiled. And then there's the sauce to consider: a rich, creamy sauce will fill you up faster than an olive oil and vegetable sauce. In any case, count on 50 to 75 grams per person if serving as a starter and 100 to 125 grams as a main course.

Spaghetti etiquette

Spaghetti – actually all pasta – should be eaten with a fork. There's no need for a knife; trying to cut up the noodles will only get you some strange looks! Italians pay attention to which pasta goes with which sauce, so if a long pasta variety is being served, then it should be the right kind for that sauce (if the sauce called for short pasta, that's what you would have found on your plate). All the trouble of getting the noodles just right will come to nothing if you start slicing them up first thing, which shows little respect in the first place. Using your fork, simply pull a couple strands of spaghetti off to an empty corner of the plate and twist these around the prongs. It takes a little practice to get the right amount on there, but you will learn.

Perfect Marriages

Combining the right pasta with the right sauce or vice-versa might seem somewhat complicated, but makes a huge difference. These combinations are generally very logical. The pasta must be able to hold the sauce well without either one overwhelming the other. In general that means: fine, thin sauces for thin noodles and thick, chunky sauces for thicker noodles. Try it out if you want: a thick sauce with large pieces of meat does not stick well to thin noodles. It slides right off. This means you will end up with nothing but sauce on your plate. *This is why spaghetti alla Bolognese is really not such a great combination.* For a meat sauce like bolognese Italians eat tagliatelle or pappardelle or short, hollow noodles. Thin sauces with an olive oil or tomato base, as often eaten in the south, are much better suited to spaghetti and other thin pastas. Northern sauces are often much heartier, containing a good deal of cheese, cream and butter. Fresh, silky egg pasta goes great with such sauces because it holds them so well. Some classic sauces have a set companion, such as *fettuccine all'Alfredo, trenette alla Genovese, pappardelle alla lepre…* golden combinations which ask for no improvement.

The plate

Without a doubt, the best thing to serve pasta in is a pre-warmed deep plate. The concave shape of the dish will retain the heat for a longer period of time. It's also a lot easier and quicker to eat out of without making a mess and splattering your dinner guests with sauce!

The cheese

Grated cheese, usually Parmesan, is often put on the table for sprinkling over the pasta. Some dishes are just not complete without it, such as *tagliatelle alla Bolognese, fettuccine all'Alfredo* or *penne alla carbonara.* For pasta dishes containing mushrooms, though, that extra cheese is usually not necessary. The same goes for fish and seafood pastas. Whatever the case, use only freshly grated cheese, never the ready-to-serve kind sold in shakers, which tastes nothing like real Parmesan.

Il primo…or not

In Italy, pasta is considered not a meal in itself but rather the first course (il primo). In the rest of the world pasta is usually served as the main course, or as a component of the main course. Pasta with a fresh, uncomplicated sauce is ideal as a quick and healthy meal during the week, perhaps with a salad on the side. And what could be tastier than a generous portion of well-seasoned pasta with a nice cut of grilled meat or good fish?

On the other hand, it is perfectly in keeping with Italian tradition to make an entire meal out of a soup. A rich minestrone, filled with vegetables and pasta, is a complete evening meal. There are plenty of options, whether you're following the 'rules' or heading out on your own.

You still find them occasionally, especially in the Italian countryside: true Italian cooks still making their own pasta fresh each day. They make it look as if there were nothing simpler in the world. In any case, they demonstrate that you don't need much to make perfect pasta. They spread flour over a large work surface, break the eggs into it and

Kitchen tools

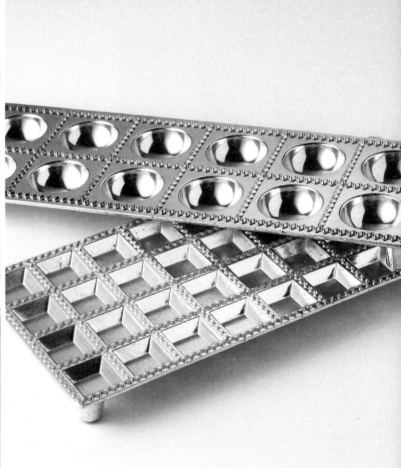

start kneading. They roll the dough out with a long wooden rolling pin. And the shape of the pasta? Roll out the dough, cut it into strips and you have tagliatelle or pappardelle. Cut it into small pieces and shape them with your thumb into little bowls: orecchiette. Cut out rectangles and pinch the middle together: farfalle.

Perhaps it does require life-long practice to do it perfectly and with total ease. But a simple pasta machine, which rolls the dough into an even sheet and cuts it too, can be a good investment for beginners. There are quite a few other things which make past making, cooking and even eating a lot easier and a whole lot more fun.

Ravioli stamps

You can use individual ravioli stamps, similar to cookie cutters, to get nice even pieces. They are available in different sizes, both square and round.

Pasta measure

This is a flat board with a series of holes, each of a different size. The proper proportion of uncooked spaghetti for a certain number of people will pass through each hole.

Rolling pins

A rolling pin is the one tool that you truly cannot do without for making fresh pasta. In Italy a long thin stick is used, sometimes 80 centimetres in length and up to five centimetres in diameter. The middle part of some versions is thicker than the ends, which taper off on both sides.

Pasta machine

Just about every specialty cooking store will stock one of these mechanical pasta makers. The simplest are quite affordable and almost indispensable if you want to make a variety of fresh pasta. The design has been completely unchanged for decades: adjustable rollers are affixed to one side of the machine, allowing you to roll out a piece of dough thinner and thinner until you have a long, even sheet. Cutting plates are positioned on the other side. These are used to cut the dough into ribbons of various widths, usually tagliatelle and tagliarine (narrow tagliatelle). The handle is equipped with additional cutters which you can use to make pappardelle or ravioli, among other things.

Pasta press

There are also semi-professional electric pasta machines on the market. Rather than rolling the dough out, they press it into various shapes. This lets you make more complicated shapes at home, such as spaghetti, maccheroni, penne rigate and fusilli. Some of these machines even mix and knead the dough for you; the only thing you have to do is put in the ingredients (and make a sauce).

Drying rack

A special drying rack comes in handy if you want to dry your own pasta. At a pinch, you can always set up a broom handle between two chairs, although a drying rack would take up a little less space.

Dough wheel

Pasta wheels are designed for cutting lasagne or tagliattelle, among other things. Some wheels give the pasta wavy or perforated edges. You can also use it to cut ravioli.

Ravioli trays

Ravioli trays come in all different shapes. You lay a sheet of dough on the top and stuff the filling into the openings, over which you lay a second sheet. Simply pass a rolling pin over the top and the dough is cut off clean against the raised edges of the tray. This will give you nice, even ravioli of an equal size. Make sure you can fill the tray without ending up with air in the ravioli afterwards (a rectangular tray with round holes for stuffing is much handier in this regard than one with, say, triangular ravioli forms). The edge must be high and sharp enough for the dough to be cut off clean. The ravioli parcels must also be easy to remove from the holes, otherwise you will be spending more time trying to pry them out.

The navel of Venus

There is an old legend describing the invention of tortellini, those delicately stuffed little rings of dough. Venus, the Roman goddess of love, and Jupiter had a secret rendezvous at an inn. The innkeeper was so impressed by Venus' beauty that he tried to spy on her while she was in the room waiting for Jupiter. He peeked at her through the keyhole as she lay on the bed. All he could see through the tiny keyhole, though, was her belly button. The perfection of that navel inspired the innkeeper to make the first 'tortellina'

Pots

Whatever pot you decide upon, the most important thing is that it's big enough. Pasta must always be cooked in plenty of water. If you plan on cooking 500 grams of pasta at a time, then you need a pot to hold five litres of water – without overflowing when you give it a good stir. A light material such as aluminium is ideal, as the pot must be easily lifted and drained when filled with several litres of boiling water.

Special pasta pots with a perforated inserts are extremely useful. The pasta is simply boiled in the insert for easy removal and straining afterwards. This is a lot handier than pouring the pasta out with the water, especially with larger quantities. You should also retain some of the pasta water, which Italians often use to thin the sauce a little.

Some 'pasta pots' are just a regular pot with no inserts, but with a perforated lid which, when the pot is tipped, can be used as a strainer. Many of these, however, do not let the water out fast enough, and are a far cry from a 'real' pasta pot.

Colander

Anyone who does not have a real pasta pot can also use a sturdy colander or other strainer just as well.

Spaghetti tester

What will they come up with next? With this little tool, you can easily fish a single strand of spaghetti out of the water to test if it's cooked. That spaghetti strand will never slide off your fork again.

Spoons and pasta ladles

These have toothed rims which hold pasta and keep long noodles from sliding off.

Bowls and plates

Pasta is best served from a large, pre-warmed bowl which can be passed around the table, or on individual deep plates or shallow bowls.

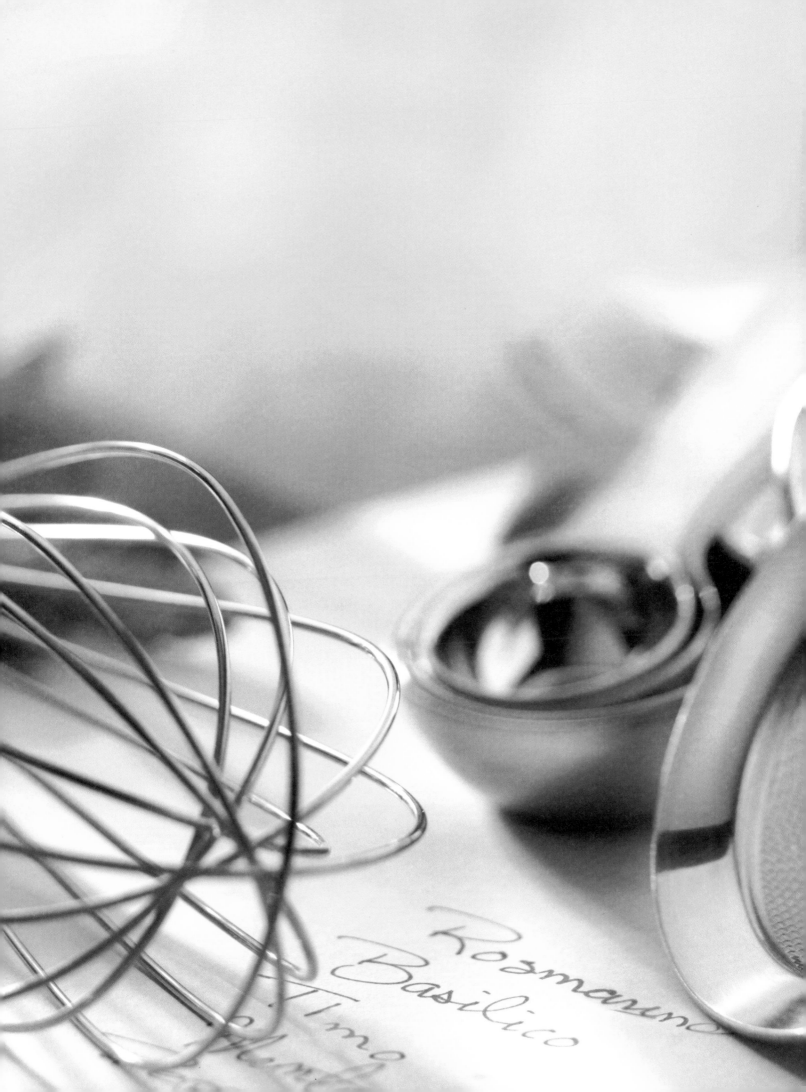

Gli spaghetti amano la compagnia, as they say in Italy, meaning 'pasta loves company'. This means that if you want to cook good pasta, you have to keep an eye on it. This way you make sure that it doesn't overcook (in Italy, overcooked pasta is considered ruined: there's nothing to do but toss it out and start over) and you can stir it now and again to keep it from lumping.

*F*ettuccine all'Alfredo, spaghetti aglio e olio, tagliatelle alla Bolognese... some pasta dishes are so unique and popular that they have become immortalised. They are enjoyed all over the world and often come in dozens or even hundreds of different versions, often with all sorts of local modifications. The question of what the truest, most authentic version of carbonara or napoletana is, is for example, the

Classics

subject of endless discussion. And perhaps all the creativity and passion these dishes seem to unleash are precisely what makes them classics.

The one noticeable constant of classic dishes is their simplicity. *Spaghetti aglio e olio* is exactly what the name suggests: spaghetti, garlic and olive oil. Even a time-consuming dish like lasagne al forno consists of relatively simple ingredients. If you plan on inventing a successful pasta recipe, it seems best to not look too far for ingredients. And have you ever wondered who that Alfredo guy really was, why ravioli di magro is not so good for your figure, or why nobody in Bologna ever eats spaghetti bolognese? For as far as possible the recipes that follow are accompanied by the story behind their creation.

Tagliatelle alla Bolognese

Ordering spaghetti bolognese in Bologna is asking for trouble. In the best-case scenario the waiter will explain to you, with scarcely suppressed indignation, that these two things just don't go together. Italians would not consider combining a thick *ragù with a thin pasta as spaghetti, as* it would simply slide off as soon as you tried to twist it around your fork. Tagliatelle is much more appropriate for holding bolognese sauce. That this sauce is most often eaten with spaghetti outside of Italy is simply because this used to be (and perhaps still is) the most readily available pasta variety, and the rich mincemeat and vegetable melange the most popular sauce. This type of sauce is made in almost all regions of Italy, usually simply called ragù. The version from Bologna, however, is by far the most famous.

300g (10oz) minced beef

1 tbsp olive oil

100g (3.5oz) pancetta, in strips

2 onions, minced

1 carrot, diced

3 celery stalks, chopped

generous handful of parsley, finely chopped

2 tbsp tomato puree

1 tin peeled Italian tomatoes (400g or 14oz)

250ml (1 cup) vegetable stock

200ml (7oz) dry white wine

1 bay leaf

salt and pepper

pinch of sugar

400g (14oz) tagliatelle all'uovo (Grand'Italia)

100g (3.5oz) chicken liver (optional)

2 tsp. butter

1. Fry the ground beef in the hot oil, stirring to keep it fine. Add the pancetta and onion and sauté until brown, stirring frequently.
2. Add the chunks of carrot and pieces of celery and cook a few minutes longer.
3. Stir in the parsley, tomato puree, peeled tomatoes, vegetable bouillon, white wine, bay leaf, salt and pepper and a pinch of sugar. Bring to a boil, then turn down the flame and let the bolognese sauce simmer gently for about 30 minutes.
4. When the sauce is close to done, cook the tagliatelle until al dente in a large pot of boiling salted water.
5. Optional: while the tagliatelle boils, cook, in another pan, the chicken liver in the butter until brown on each side. Remove from the pan and chop finely. Stir the chopped chicken liver into the sauce.
6. Strain the tagliatelle and mix it directly into the sauce. Serve immediately.

The nutritional value of many vegetables is severely reduced through cooking. The health benefits of tomatoes, on the other hand, are actually enhanced. By cutting and heating tomatoes, the body can more readily absorb the fruit's inherent lycopene, an antioxidant. Lycopene is regarded as an absolute boon for many things: it is said to have anti-inflammatory properties for sufferers of heart disease, preventative effects for certain kinds of cancer, protection against macula degeneration (an eye disease) and to be good against osteoporosis. No time to make tomato sauce from scratch? Then just replace that tin of peeled tomatoes and the tomato puree in this recipe with a bottle of Sugocasa Tradizionale (Grand'Italia). Sugocasa is a good, pure alternative. The tomatoes are processed within 24 hours of harvest and contain no artificial additives.

Penne alla carbonara

Few pasta dishes are the subject of such fervent discussion as carbonara. With parsley or without, garlic or no garlic, long or short pasta, and (the hottest topic of all) cream or no cream? Usually the Italian version is served without cream and some people regard that addition as wrong or unauthentic at best. There was a time when some Italian versions of this recipe did get a dash of cream, especially if they were being cooked for people who needed their strength, after an illness, say. In any case, the Sicilian coal miners after whom this dish is named certainly needed some hearty food after a long day underground. They are said to have made this dish quite often because it requires few ingredients and can easily be thrown together over a camp fire. A generous sprinkling of freshly ground black pepper on the plate is reminiscent of the flecks of coal which fell from the miners' clothes as they ate.

1. Cook the penne until al dente in a large pot of boiling salted water.
2. While the pasta cooks, sauté the pancetta in a pan together with the garlic.
3. Remove the garlic.
4. Strain the penne and mix into the pancetta. Remove the pan from the heat.
5. Stir the eggs and grated pecorino into the penne and keep stirring until the eggs become creamy. Add salt and freshly ground black pepper to taste. Serve immediately.

400g (14oz) penne rigate (Grand'Italia)
salt
250g (9oz) pancetta, chopped
1 clove of garlic, peeled
200g (7oz) pecorino, grated
2 eggs, beaten
salt and freshly ground black pepper

ⓥ Spaghetti alla Napoletana

The Neapolitans were among the first Europeans to use tomatoes, brought back from South America by Spanish explorers, for culinary purposes. This was a revolutionary idea. The rest of Italy was growing tomato plants at this time – but only as an ornamental! Simply made and briefly cooked tomato sauce (even without the garlic and basil) is still known as napoletana. This sauce is not only used for pasta and to season vegetables, it's also what comes on top of your pizza.

1. Heat the oil in a frying pan and sauté the onion until translucent.
   Add the tomatoes, chilli powder, a little salt and a pinch of sugar. Stir well and simmer gently on low heat for 5 minutes.
2. Cook the spaghetti until al dente in a large pot of boiling salted water.
3. Strain the spaghetti and mix it directly into the sauce together with the chopped parsley and basil.
4. Portion on to plates or into bowls and sprinkle with Parmesan cheese. Serve immediately.

2 tbsp olive oil
1 onion, minced
400g (14oz) tomatoes, seeded and diced
small pinch of hot chilli powder
salt
a little sugar
400g (14oz) spaghetti
small handful of parsley, coarsely chopped
small handful of basil, coarsely chopped
50g Parmesan cheese, coarsely grated

Bucatini con le sarde

The origin of this typical Sicilian dish most likely lies in the Middle Ages, a time when the island was under Arab rule. Some say they were the ones who taught the Sicilians the art of pasta making. Whatever the case may be, this sauce is a wonderful fusion of locally available ingredients and Arabic influences. The long, hollow pasta (bucatini or maccharoni) and sardines, fresh from the surrounding waters of the Mediterranean, are seasoned with the island's wild fennel, Arabian saffron, lemon zest, raisins and pine nuts. The Sicilian cook, Pino Correnti, warns us to keep this recipe from the 'tomato rain', which is the tendency to throw tomato into any pasta sauce without a second thought. Saffron, he says, is perfectly sufficient for achieving the proper colour.

500g (18oz) fresh sardines, cleaned, heads and bones removed

salt

juice and grated peel (zest) of 1 lemon

1 fennel bulb, tough centre removed and the rest cut into strips

1 tin of anchovy filets (50g or 1.75oz), chopped

3 cloves of garlic, chopped

generous handful of parsley, chopped

6 tbsp olive oil

1 tsp. fennel seed

1 onion, minced

50g (1.75oz) raisins, soaked in a little water (save the water)

small pinch of saffron, soaked in a little water

2 tbsp pine nuts, toasted in a dry pan on very low heat

400g (14oz) bucatini

freshly ground pepper

1. Pat the sardines dry and sprinkle with a little salt. Drizzle with lemon juice and set them in a cold place.

2. Cook the strips of fennel until tender, about 5 minutes. Strain in a colander (saving the liquid) and dice.

3. With a mortar and pestle, grind the anchovies, garlic, half the parsley, 4 tablespoons of olive oil, the zest of half a lemon and the fennel seed to a paste.

4. Heat 1 tablespoon of olive oil in a frying pan and briefly sauté the onion. Add the fennel pieces and continue cooking. Turn the flame down low and stir in the anchovy paste, the raisins with their water, the saffron, 1 tablespoon of fennel cooking liquid and the pine nuts. Simmer gently for a few minutes.

5. Pour the rest of the cooking liquid from the fennel into a large pot, adding extra water until you have the right amount for boiling pasta. Bring to a boil and salt. Cook the bucatini until al dente.

6. Pat the sardines dry. Heat 1 tablespoon olive oil in a second frying pan and cook the sardines on both sides until tender, about 2 minutes. Sprinkle with a little salt and freshly ground pepper

7. Strain the bucatini and divide over 4 plates. Ladle the sauce onto the pasta and place a few sardines on each serving. Garnish with the remaining parsley and serve right away.

`the MAN

which a

eats PASTA

of their

NER in
person
is an indication
CHARACTER'

(Italian saying)

Farfalle alla boscaiola

Porcini mushrooms are an indispensable ingredient in this deliciously creamy 'woodsman's *sauce'*. They lend the dish an earthy yet refined flavour. Porcini grow in the forests of Lombardy, where this sauce originates. *Pasta alla boscaiola has made its mark* all over Italy, usually made with a short pasta like farfalle or penne, sometimes with pappardelle.

1. Heat the olive oil in a pan and sauté the onion and chopped porcini for about 3 minutes or until the onion is translucent.
2. Add the garlic, fresh mushroom slices, chopped sage and a little salt and pepper. Continue cooking for about 5 minutes on medium heat, stirring frequently.
3. Pour in the liquid from the porcini and the wine and simmer on low heat.
4. Cook the farfalle until al dente in a large pot of boiling salted water.
5. While the pasta cooks, stir the mascarpone and gorgonzola into the mushroom sauce. Heat through and continue stirring until the cheese has melted. Add salt and pepper to taste.
6. Strain the farfalle and mix into the sauce.
7. Portion on to plates or into bowls and garnish with sage. Serve immediately.

2 tbsp olive oil
1 onion, finely chopped
25g (1oz) dried porcini mushrooms, soaked in hot water and chopped (drain the liquid and set aside for later)
2 cloves of garlic, pressed
400g (14oz) mixed (wild) mushrooms, thinly sliced
small handful of fresh sage, finely chopped (plus a few leaves cut into strips as garnish)
salt and freshly ground pepper
200ml (7oz) dry white wine
400g (14oz) farfalle (Grand'Italia)
120g (4oz) mascarpone
200g (7oz) gorgonzola, crumbled

Pappardelle alla lepre

Tuscany, with its wide-ranging forests, has brought us many game dishes. This hare *ragù with broad ribbon* pasta is an excellent example. The meat is marinated overnight in red wine and slowly stewed with tomatoes and vegetables until it is so tender it falls off the bone. The same dish is cooked in the Tuscan city of Lucca with rabbit rather than hare.

500g (18oz) hare meat, cleaned and sectioned
5 tbsp olive oil
1 tbsp fresh or 1 tsp. dried thyme
400g (14oz) tomatoes, seeded and cut into medium-sized chunks
salt and freshly ground pepper
2 tbsp tomato puree
400g (14oz) pappardelle
handful of parsley, chopped

For the marinade:
0.5l (2 cups) red wine
3 celery stalks, coarsely cut
2 onions, coarsely cut
3 cloves of garlic, coarsely cut
1 tsp. fennel seed
1 bay leaf
2 cloves
6 peppercorns

1. Combine all the ingredients for the marinade in a large bowl and mix in the hare meat. Cover and marinade in the refrigerator for 24 hours. Turn the meat every few hours.
2. Remove the meat from the marinade and pat dry. Strain the marinade through a sieve, discarding the peppercorns and cloves. Place the vegetables in a colander to drain, reserving the liquid for later.
3. Heat 3 tablespoons of olive oil in a frying pan and cook the meat until brown on each side. Add the vegetables from the marinade and continue cooking, stirring every few minutes.
4. Pour in the marinade and sprinkle with thyme, salt and pepper. Stew on low heat, uncovered, for about 2 hours or until tender.
5. Take the meat from the pan, remove it from the bones and cut it into small pieces.
6. Remove the bay leaf and puree the sauce with an handheld blender.
7. Stir the tomato pieces, tomato puree and the meat into the sauce and simmer on medium heat.
8. Cook the pappardelle until al dente in a large pot of boiling salted water.
9. Strain the pasta and mix into the sauce. Portion on to plates and sprinkle with parsley. Serve right away.

Trenette alla Genovese

(V)

The Genovese are a bit like the Dutch in that they are famous for their thriftiness. This might be why they started supplementing their pasta with pieces of potato and haricots – so they wouldn't have to use so much pesto! Pasta is only known as trenette in Liguria. If you can't find this variety, another small, flat ribbon pasta will work too.

2 boiling potatoes, peeled,
halved and cut lengthwise in approx. 0.5cm thick slices.
100g (3.5oz) haricots verts, halved
salt
400g (14oz) trenette

For the pesto:
generous handful of fresh basil
2 cloves of garlic, thinly sliced
1.5 tbsp pine nuts
100g (3.5oz) Parmesan cheese, grated
4 tbsp olive oil
salt

1. Blend all the ingredients for the pesto into a thick sauce with an hand-held blender.
2. Boil the potatoes and haricots in a large pot of salted water, uncovered, until tender, about 5 minutes. Remove from the pot with a skimmer or sieve and let drain.
3. Add the trenette to the water and return to a boil. Cook the pasta until al dente.
4. Scoop the pesto into a large bowl and stir in 3 to 4 tablespoons of the pasta water.
5. Strain the trenette and stir into the pesto sauce along with the potatoes and haricots. Mix well and portion on to plates. Serve immediately.

Spaghetti alle vongole

There are actually two versions of Venus clams and pasta: the 'red' kind with a tomato-based sauce and this 'white' variety with white wine, garlic and parsley. Some cooks also put a dash of cream into this version, though strictly speaking this is not authentic. Serve the vongole with linguine or spaghetti.

1kg (2.2lbs) fresh venus clams, washed (discard any open shells)
250ml (1cup) dry white wine
2 tbsp olive oil
1 small onion, minced
3 cloves of garlic, minced
generous handful of fresh parsley, minced
400g (14oz) spaghetti all'uovo (Grand'Italia)
salt
2 tbsp butter
juice of half a lemon
freshly ground pepper

1. Place the venus clams in a large pan, pour in the white wine and bring to a boil. Simmer for about 5 minutes or until the shells open (discard the ones that remain closed). Remove the clams from the pan and strain the liquid, setting it aside.
2. Heat 2 tablespoons of olive oil in a pan and sauté the onion, garlic and half of the parsley until the onion is translucent.
3. Add the cooking liquid from the clams and boil it down to half.
4. Cook the spaghetti until al dente in a large pot of boiling salted water.
5. Stir the venus clams and the butter into the reduced liquid and add lemon juice, salt and pepper to taste.
6. Strain the spaghetti and mix directly into the sauce. Portion the spaghetti alle vongole onto plates, sprinkle with parsley and a little freshly ground pepper and serve immediately.

Gnocchi alla Romana

The word gnocchi literally means 'clumps'. As you might imagine, there are several dishes which fall under this description; the most famous 'clumps' are made from potatoes. This Roman variant, however, is actually closest to the original, made from a mixture of wheat flour, eggs and water. This recipe is much older (exactly how old is unknown) than gnocchi di patate, which 'only' dates back to the eighteenth century. These hand-shaped dumplings can be baked in the oven or sautéed in a pan with some butter. A simple tomato sauce is the classic companion (see page 32).

1l (4 cups) milk
salt and pepper
60g butter plus extra
225g Italian flour (semola di grano duro)
2 eggs plus 1 egg yolk, beaten
75g Parmesan cheese, grated

1. Bring the milk to the boil and add salt and pepper to taste. Add the butter and stir until melted.
2. Stir the flour into the milk a little at a time. Keep stirring on low heat for about 15 minutes or until a thick dough has formed. Remove the pan from the heat.
3. Add the eggs, beaten, and half the cheese to the dough. Mix well. Pour the mixture into a greased casserole dish or baking sheet. Let cool.
4. Preheat the oven to 200°C (400°F or gas mark 6).
5. Using a cookie cutter, cut rounds with a diameter of approx. 3cm out of the sheet of dough and place in a greased casserole dish. Sprinkle with the Parmesan cheese and a few lumps of butter. Bake for approx. 10 minutes or until the gnocchi has a golden-brown crust.

Ravioli di magro

'Lean' ravioli? Admittedly, they aren't the best thing for your figure, what with all that delicious ricotta and buttery sauce. But di magro here does not refer to the caloric value but to the absence of meat. Since time immemorial, this type of ravioli has been eaten during the forty days of fasting prior to Easter. For many people, this is still a time of moderation, a period in which neither meat nor alcohol is consumed (or, in any case, less than usual). These ravioli are also quite tasty with a cream sauce topped with a slice of butter and a handful of Parmesan cheese.

For the pasta dough:
300g (10.5oz) Italian pasta flour (type '00'), sifted
3 eggs
half tsp. salt to taste
half tbsp olive oil

For the filling:
1 small onion, finely chopped
1 clove garlic, minced
1 tbsp olive oil
400g (14oz) spinach, coarsely chopped
300g (10.5oz) ricotta
salt and freshly ground pepper
100g (3.5oz) butter
small handful of fresh sage, cut into strips

1. Make a pile of the semolina on a clean, dry surface and form a pit in the middle. Break the eggs into the pit and sprinkle in the salt. Using a fork, carefully stir from the centre outwards until the flour is completely mixed with the liquid. Knead the dough for 10-15 minutes until it becomes soft and elastic. Cover it in plastic wrap and put aside for 30 minutes to set.

2. Meanwhile, gently sauté the onion and garlic in the oil for the filling. Stir in the spinach. As soon as it boils down, remove the pan from the heat. Strain the mixture through a sieve and scoop into a mixing bowl. Stir in the ricotta and add salt and pepper to taste.

3. Roll the dough out on a floured surface until you have a rectangular sheet less than 1cm in thickness. Imagine a line running down the middle of the sheet and place small mounds of filling on one side of this line. Moisten the dough around the filling with a wet brush. Fold the sheet double and gently press the dough together around the filling. Separate the ravioli, using a pastry wheel or sharp knife. Crimp the edges together with the prongs of a fork.

4. Using a ravioli cutter, press half-moons or squares out of the dough, or use a pastry wheel to cut the ravioli. Cook the ravioli in plenty of boiling water for 3 to 4 minutes. Strain.

5. Meanwhile, melt the butter together with the strips of sage on low heat. Do not let the butter brown.

6. Portion on to plates and pour the sage butter over the top. Serve immediately.

Lasagne al forno

One of the earliest milestones in the history of Italian pasta has to do with lasagne, or laganon, as recorded by a historian in the 1st century AD. Layers of dough were baked with a filling of meat or fish in between. Centuries later, this ancient recipe has evolved into innumerable, delicious varieties, though the best known is still this version with *ragù* and béchamel sauce. It's tastiest when made fresh at home, including the lasagne (lasagne being the plural of lasagna, which refers to a single sheet of pasta). The ingredients are simple, but must be fresh and of the best quality.

1 tbsp olive oil
400g (14oz) ground beef
2 cloves garlic, chopped
1 onion, chopped
1 carrot, cut into small chunks
small handful of parsley, chopped
2 tbsp tomato puree
200ml (7oz) vegetable stock
1 package green lasagne leaves (500 g), pre-cooked if necessary (most brands do not require pre-cooking).
1 tbsp butter
100g (3.5oz) Parmesan cheese, grated

For the béchamel sauce:
60g (2oz) butter
60g (2oz) wheat flour
1l (4 cups) whole milk, warm
salt and pepper
pinch of ground nutmeg

1. Preheat the oven to 180°C (350° F or gas mark 4).
2. Heat the olive oil in a pan and sauté the ground beef, stirring to keep it fine. Add the garlic, onion, pieces of carrot and parsley and continue cooking on high heat for approx. 2 minutes. Stir in the tomato puree and continue cooking.
3. Pour the bouillon into the meat mixture, stir well and bring to a boil. Turn down the flame and simmer gently for 30 minutes.
4. Meanwhile, melt the butter for the béchamel sauce in a pan and heat until it foams up. Add the flour and whisk well. Continue whisking until the mixture (now roux) has a smooth, firm consistency. This takes several minutes. The roux should not stick or crisp up but turn a light golden colour (not too dark).
5. Remove the pan from the heat and pour in the warm milk a little at a time. Continue stirring well to prevent it becoming lumpy.
6. Return the pan to the heat and add salt and pepper and a pinch of nutmeg to taste. Cook the béchamel sauce, stirring constantly, for about 5 minutes. Remove from the heat and set aside for later.
7. Place a layer of lasagne leaves on the bottom of a greased casserole dish. Spoon a layer of meat sauce over the leaves, followed by a layer of béchamel sauce. Continue layering in this order, ending with the béchamel. Top with the Parmesan cheese.
8. Bake the lasagna for 30 minutes or until golden brown.

Bucatini all'Amatriciana

This piquant bacon sauce did not originate in Rome, as once believed, but in the mountain town of Amatrice on the border between Latium and Abruzzi. The shepherds who lived in these mountains made pasta sauce from ingredients which were easily preserved and could be taken on long journeys: hard sheep's cheese, chilli peppers and dried bacon. The official version (so official it's even been laid down by the municipal government!) *calls for guanciale*, or pork jowl. Pancetta is a good substitute, though purists will tell you this is not true, authentic Amatriciana. Leave out the onion and garlic too, they don't belong in here either. It's best served with bucatini, spaghetti or vermicelli.

200g (7oz) streaky bacon or pork belly
(preferably Italian guanciale or pancetta), cubed
2 tbsp olive oil
1 dried chilli pepper (peperoncini), crumbled
500g (18oz) tomatoes, seeded and diced
400g (14oz) bucatini
salt
50g (1.75oz) Parmesan cheese, grated
50g (1.75oz) pecorino, grated

1. Cook the pork in a dry frying pan until crisp. Pour off the excess fat and replace it with 2 tablespoons of olive oil.
2. Stir in the chilli pepper and tomatoes and continue sautéing until it has cooked down to a thick sauce.
3. Cook the bucatini until al dente in a large pot of boiling salted water.
4. Strain the bucatini and mix into the tomato sauce.
5. Portion into bowls and sprinkle with the grated cheeses. Serve immediately.

Olive oil

Gnarled trees with grey-green leaves, flowing in long rows across the rolling landscape. Is there a more Italian scene? Olive orchards grow over almost all of Italy. The country is the world's second-largest olive oil producer, after Spain.

The olive harvest is fascinating to observe. In large part, it is still done by hand, due to the fact that it's quite difficult to remove the olives from the branches by machine without damaging them. They must be picked before fully ripe. This gives you the highest quality oil, though it makes for difficult picking – unripe olives don't like to leave their branches. If bruised, this has an adverse effect on the flavour. This is why olive harvesters spread nets out under the trees and carefully 'rake' the fruit off with a special kind of stick. Once they're harvested, the olives are crushed and turned into that special 'golden nectar' as quickly as possible.

Vergine and vierge

Litres and litres of olive oil pass through Italian kitchens each year. Most households always have at least two kinds, a good vergine or extra vergine oil and a 'normal' olive oil. Though derived from the same fruit, the two varieties are quite different. The names used to refer to the method of production. Vergine (or vierge, as the French would have it) came from the first 'cold' pressing, after which the remaining pulp was heated and pressed once again. These days, centrifuges are used, which get almost all the oil out of the olives. The name, however, has remained as a designation of quality.

Extra virgin now refers to a maximum acidity of one percent. This is the purest and most flavourful oil. Virgin oil contains less than two percent acidity. Together, these unprocessed oils account for around ten percent of total olive oil production. The rest is made up of oils which are refined to remove their high acidity or other impurities. This extra processing leads to a reduction in flavour, though it does have one benefit: such oils can be heated to higher temperatures, making them better suited as cooking oil. Virgin and extra virgin olive oil are best used cold, in dressings and dips, for example. Such oil will lose its delicate flavour as soon as it's heated. Sautéing with extra virgin olive oil is a culinary sin!

Peppery or fruity

Good olive oil has all sorts of subtle flavours, which are determined by the variety of olive, the ripeness of the fruit and the manner of production, among other factors. Oil from Tuscany is often peppery in flavour, while the Ligurian varieties taste mild and fruity and Sicilian olive oil packs a real punch, with a rich, nutty taste.

ⓥ Spaghetti con aglio e olio

This recipe from Rome goes to show that good pasta does not need a lot of extras. It is perfect in its simplicity and contains exactly what the name says: spaghetti, garlic and olive oil. Another variant is spaghetti *aglio, olio e peperoncino, for which a dried chilli pepper is sautéed along with the garlic* (and removed right before serving), lending the dish some extra heat. This dish is even eaten without cheese.

400g (14oz) spaghetti (Grand'Italia)
salt
10 cloves of garlic, thinly sliced
2 tbsp olive oil

1. Cook the spaghetti until al dente in a large pot of boiling salted water.
2. While the pasta cooks, heat the oil in a frying pan and sauté the garlic on low heat for about 2 minutes or until golden brown.
3. Strain the spaghetti and toss with the garlic. Serve immediately.

Hangover remedy

Many Italians swear by it: a big plate of spaghetti con aglio, *olio e peperoncino* (spaghetti with garlic, oil and chilli pepper) after an evening of a bit too much wine. The consumption of carbohydrates is thought to help break down the alcohol in your body while the oil leaves a coating on the stomach wall which is said to cure that awful upset feeling. Pain-killing qualities have been attributed to garlic as well as chilli peppers. It's worth a shot, anyway.

Fettuccine all'Alfredo

(v)

The Alfredo who immortalised this delightfully simple pasta creation was called Alfredo di Lelio. He was a restaurateur in Rome in the 1920s. One of the many stories about the history of this dish, a variation on fettuccine al burro (with butter), is that he prepared it for his pregnant wife, who had little appetite at the time. In particular, the large amount of butter – even more generous than the original recipe called for – made it extra nourishing (and tasty). In his restaurant, the clever Alfredo served this dish to celebrities with a golden fork. This, more than anything else, is probably what made it famous in the first place. The funny thing is, in Italy it is still usually known simply as fettuccine al burro or al doppio burro (with double butter).

100g (3.5oz) butter
200ml (7oz) single cream or panna da cucina
50g (1.75oz) Parmesan cheese, grated + extra for sprinkling
400g (14oz) fettuccine
salt and pepper

1. Melt the butter in a large pan and pour in the cream. Bring to a boil and immediately lower the flame. Simmer gently for 5 minutes, stirring constantly. Add the Parmesan cheese and stir until a smooth sauce results. Remove from the heat.
2. Cook the fettuccine until al dente in a large pot of boiling salted water.
3. Return the cheese sauce to low heat. Strain the fettuccine and stir into the cheese sauce. Add salt and pepper to taste.
4. Portion the fettuccine all'Alfredo onto plates or into bowls and sprinkle with freshly grated Parmesan cheese. Serve immediately.

Minestrone

The base of this dish has always been a good, clear homemade stock. Beyond that, the ingredients for minestrone diverge greatly depending on the region, the season, the person or the mood... Leftovers from the day before often find their way into the soup. Hence the name: minestra means 'mixture'. In Calabria it's called millecosedde, the soup of 'a thousand things'. All possible vegetables and legumes can be incorporated into minestrone and the types of pasta also vary a good deal, from vermicelli and many small varieties (pastine) to short, thick pasta like penne. A little grated cheese over the top will thicken it up a bit. Or follow the Ligurian example and put a scoop of pesto in there.

1 large potato, diced
1 carrot, thinly sliced
1 onion, cut into rings
1 leek, cut into rings
1 clove of garlic, finely chopped
3 tbsp olive oil
1.5l vegetable stock
100g (3.5oz) mafaldine
100g (3.5oz) green peas
100g (3.5oz) cannellini beans (tinned)
2 tomatoes, cut into chunks
handful of fresh parsley, finely chopped
salt and pepper

1. Sauté the potato, carrot, onion, leek and garlic for a few minutes in the olive oil.
2. Add the stock and simmer gently for 15 minutes, allowing the flavours to combine.
3. Add the pasta, green peas, cannellini beans, tomato and parsley and continue simmering for 5 minutes or until the pasta is just tender.
4. Add salt and pepper to taste.
5. Pour the minestrone into bowls or deep plates and serve.

Here's a recipe for a quick and delicious homemade vegetable stock. Sauté 2 large onions, thinly sliced; 1 large carrot, cut into chunks; half a bunch of celery, cut into chunks; a sprig of celery leaves; and 1 leek, thinly sliced, in a tablespoon of olive oil. Add 1.5 litres of water, bring to the boil and simmer for 20 minutes on low heat. Drain the stock and add salt to taste.

"It will be maccheroni, I swear to you, that will unite Italy!"

An impassioned declaration by Giuseppe Garibaldi, the national hero who fought to make the fragmented country a single nation in the nineteenth century. In Garibaldi's time, pasta was one of the few things that all the independent states of Italy had in common.

RISTORANTE
pasta - caffé

Spaghetti alla puttanesca

There is no mistaking where this delicious pasta dish from Campania gets its name: alla puttanesca means 'of the whores'. Some claim that the sauce's seductive aroma filled the air, drawing men to the house of these women of ill repute. Others maintain the name comes from the fact that it is so easy to prepare, it could be squeezed in between two 'clients'!

400g (14oz) spaghetti
salt
2 tbsp olive oil
2 cloves of garlic, thinly sliced
1 can of anchovy filets (50g or 1.75oz), finely chopped
1kg (2.2lbs) ripe tomatoes, finely chopped
100g (3.5oz) black olives, pitted
small handful of parsley, minced
1 tbsp capers

1. Cook the spaghetti until al dente in a large pot of boiling salted water.
2. While the pasta cooks, heat the oil in a large pan, add the garlic and anchovy and continue cooking, stirring constantly, until the anchovy has 'melted'.
3. Add the tomato to the anchovy paste and stir this mixture over high heat until it has cooked down to a thick sauce. Reduce the heat and stir in the olives, parsley and capers.
4. Strain the spaghetti and mix it directly into the tomato sauce.
5. Portion into deep plates and serve immediately

Ⓥ Spaghetti alla marinara

This is typically one of those sauces about which there is a good deal of confusion. Is it a sauce with mussels and other seafood or is it just a very simple tomato sauce? Because of the word marinara, derived from marinaro, or 'seaman', you would expect there to be some kind of fish or seafood in it. Au contraire. Traditionally, this tomato sauce – that's really all it is – is prepared for Neapolitan mariners returning from their time at sea. No mussels, no seafood at all, not even anchovies. This strictly vegan sauce is one of the few tomato sauces that is served without cheese. In certain countries, if you see marinara on the menu it's referring to some kind of seafood pasta. This is due to the large number of Italian immigrants who set up eateries all over the world shortly after WWII but who didn't have the best knowledge of traditional Italian recipes. The misnomered versions were quickly adopted, becoming new classics in their host countries.

6 tbsp olive oil

500g (18oz) ripe tomatoes, peeled, seeded and cut into thin strips

1 small red chilli pepper, seeded and minced

2 cloves of garlic, very thinly sliced

1 tbsp capers

400g (14oz) spaghetti

salt

3 tbsp fresh parsley, chopped

100g (3.5oz) large black olives, pitted and sliced into ringlets

1. Heat 1 tablespoon of olive oil in a pan and sauté the strips of tomato on low heat for about 5 minutes or until softened.

2. Heat 2 tablespoons of the olive oil in another large, deep pan and add the chilli pepper and garlic. Continue cooking for another minute, stirring constantly.

3. Add the tomatoes, the remaining olive oil and the capers and cook for a further 2-3 minutes, stirring constantly.

4. Meanwhile, cook the spaghetti until al dente in a large pot of boiling salted water.

5. Strain the spaghetti and mix it directly into the tomato sauce, together with the parsley and olive ringlets. Keep on the heat for a final minute, still stirring. Portion onto plates and serve immediately.

Pesto alla Genovese

Liguria, the narrow coastal province in the far northwest of Italy, is blessed with a bounty of wild basil. Many people are convinced that nowhere else in the world does this herb taste as good as here. The shiny green leaves have a uniquely intense flavour and aroma. They say it comes from the wind blowing in from the sea...

This region, with its wealth of herbs, is home to the world's most famous basil blend: pesto. For thousands of years Ligurians have been crushing the leaves of this herb to a fine paste, together with the rich-tasting local olive oil, garlic and pecorino, that deliciously crumbly Italian sheep's cheese. Pine nuts were added to the recipe at some time, lending the mixture an intensely creamy texture.

The old mortar and pestle

Pesto is traditionally made in a stone mortar, crushed to a paste with a heavy pestle. This *is also where the name comes from – pestare is the Italian verb 'to* crush'. Though, of course, you can always throw everything in the food processor, the old-fashioned way of making pesto is perhaps still the best. The blunt force of the pestle creates a beautifully smooth texture, while the food processor merely turns everything into little pieces. Crush all the ingredients, except the cheese and olive oil, to a fine paste, stir in the grated cheese and add the olive oil last, mixing it all to a thick sauce.

Hundreds of varieties

There are numerous variants of the original Italian pesto. Just about every cook has his own recipe. The best-known 'alternative' pesto is the kind made from sun-dried tomatoes, *pesto rosso*. Rocket is also frequently used in place of the basil – or other tender, aromatic herbs, or vegetables like roasted peppers or aubergine, other types of cheese, walnuts or almonds, different nut oils...

The most famous pesto dish is trenette alla Genovese – a thin ribbon pasta with green pesto and boiled potatoes and haricots. Ligurians also eat their famous herb mixture on gnocchi and in minestrone. The possibilities are almost infinite. Try spreading pesto on crostini (toasted bread slices), with salad or as a sauce for meat or fish.

A hot, steaming pot of beef marrows, fresh vegetables and herbs has been quietly bubbling away on a low flame for hours, spreading a glorious aroma through the whole house, simmering down to a thick and savoury nectar. It is often served with nothing more than some small pasta forms. Such a wonderful bouillon needs little else. Sometimes the cook will throw in some green peas, meatballs or pieces of braised chicken liver. However you serve it, pasta in brodo always needs a lovingly prepared broth. Pasta soups play a large role in Italian cuisine. Usually they are served as the primo instead of pastasciutta, or pasta with sauce. There are hundreds of small pasta varieties (pastine) specially designed for soup, from simple risi or peperini – named after rice and peppercorns because of their shape – to all

Pasta soups

sorts of smaller versions of well-known pastas. There are farfallette ('little butterflies' or 'little bowties'), orecchiettini ('little ears'), tubetti ('little pipes'), conchigliette ('little shells')... etc. Of course, the famous alphabet soup pasta, alfabetini, are especially adored by children. Tortellini and gnocchi also make their way into clear broths now and again.

Minestrone is thicker and packed with fresh vegetables, legumes and all sorts of pasta. When served with some nice crusty bread, this hearty soup is a meal in itself – a great lunch for a chilly day. Such a bowl of heart-warming fresh soup will quickly replenish that much-needed energy.

All of the following recipes make four servings.

ⓥ Spinach soup with mini noodles

1l (4 cups) vegetable stock
100g (3.5oz) small soup pasta (farfalline or stelline, etc.)
500g (18oz) spinach, rinsed and chopped
2 tbsp cooking cream
salt
whole grain bread, on the side

1. Bring the stock to the boil.
2. Cook the pasta in the stock. When it is al dente, remove it with a skimmer or sieve. Rinse briefly under cold water from the tap and set aside for later.
3. Stir the spinach into the stock and let it boil down briefly.
4. Puree the soup with a hand-held blender.
5. Stir the cream and the pasta into the spinach soup. Heat through before ladling into bowls. Serve with whole grain bread.

Beef bouillon with spaghettini and meatballs

100g (3.5oz) Parmesan cheese, coarsely grated
1 egg
1 tbsp bread crumbs
salt and pepper
250g (9oz) mincemeat
1l (4 cups) beef bouillon
100g spaghettini
small handful of parsley, minced

1. To make the meatballs, stir half the Parmesan cheese, the egg, bread crumbs and a little salt and pepper into the mincemeat. Shape the mixture into small balls with your hands.
2. Bring the bouillon to the boil and add the meat balls and the spaghettini. Simmer on low heat for 4-5 minutes or until the meatballs are cooked through and the pasta is al dente.
3. Portion the soup into 4 shallow bowls, sprinkle with the remaining cheese and the parsley and serve immediately.

Always buy spinach as fresh as possible, wrap it loosely in newspaper and store in your refrigerator's vegetable drawer. Do not keep for more than a day or two.

You will find shaping meatballs is a lot easier if you wet your hands first.

Fresh tomato soup
with orecchiette

1 tbsp olive oil
1 small onion, minced
1 celery stalk, thinly sliced
1 clove garlic, peeled
1kg (18oz) ripe tomatoes, seeded and diced
1l (4 cups) vegetable stock
100g (3.5oz) orecchiette
ciabatta, on the side

1. Heat the oil in a pan and sauté the onion, celery and garlic until the onion is translucent.
2. Add the chopped tomatoes and continue sautéing for another minute, stirring constantly.
3. Pour in the stock and bring to the boil. Reduce the heat to a simmer and cook, uncovered, for approx. 20 minutes.
4. Puree the soup with a hand-held blender or in a traditional blender. Strain through a sieve. Return to the heat and bring to the boil.
5. Add the orecchiette and simmer gently for a few more minutes or until the pasta is al dente. Serve with ciabatta.

Just like the potato, chilli pepper, maize and tobacco, the tomato also originated in South America. This fruit is a member of the nightshade family, a group of plants which once suffered from a very bad reputation. The green parts of the plant do, indeed, contain poisonous alkaloids which can be deadly when consumed in large amounts. When the tomato first made its way to Europe, it was adopted as an ornamental. The first tomatoes cultivated for food in Europe were a small, yellow variety grown in Italy, where they were called 'golden apples' or pomo d'oro. This name is still used in Italian, the only difference being that the two words are now written as one: pomodoro.

Bouillon with green peas and pancetta

ⓥ Vegetable soup with tortellini

1 tbsp olive oil

1 onion, chopped

1 celery stalk, thinly sliced

1 clove garlic, minced

1 tbsp tomato puree

1l (4 cups) beef bouillon

200g (7oz) pappardelle

100g (3.5oz) pancetta, diced

500g (18oz) green peas (frozen)

small handful of parsley, minced

1. Heat the oil in a large pan and sauté the onion, celery and garlic until the onion is translucent.
   Stir in the tomato puree and let this cook for a few seconds.
2. Pour in the bouillon and bring to the boil.
3. Add the pappardelle and cook until al dente.
4. When the pappardelle are 3 minutes from being done, stir in the green peas, pancetta and parsley.
5. Portion into shallow bowls and serve immediately.

1l (4 cups) vegetable stock

100g (3.5oz) haricots verts,
 cut into small segments

1 small carrot, in chunks

1 celery stalk, thinly sliced

1 beefsteak tomato, or other large
stewing variety, seeded
and diced.

100g (3.5oz) broccoli, in small florets

small handful of celery leaf, minced

250g (9oz) cheese tortellini (home-made or
fresh from the supermarket)

salt and pepper

1. Bring the stock to the boil and add the haricots, carrot and celery stalk.
2. Cook for 5 minutes, then add the tomato, broccoli, celery leaf and tortellini. Keep on the heat for another 2 minutes or until the tortellini are al dente
3. Ladle the soup into shallow bowls and serve immediately.

Tomatoes are best peeled by first carving a cross in the bottom with a sharp knife. Drop them one by one into a pot of boiling water until the skin starts to curl. Immediately remove them from the pot and rinse under cold water from the tap. The skin should now slip off with ease.

Tortellini in brodo rosso

1 tbsp olive oil
1 onion, minced
2 cloves garlic, minced
1 tbsp sugar
100ml (3.5oz) red wine
900ml (3.5 cups) chicken stock
1 carrot, thinly sliced
1 leek, cut into half-circles
1 celery stalk, sliced
200g (7oz) tortellini alla carne (Grand'Italia)
100g (3.5oz) Parmesan cheese
small handful of fresh oregano, cut into strips
bunch of chives, minced

1. Heat the oil in a pan and sauté the onion and garlic for 1 minute.
2. Sprinkle with sugar and keep on low heat, stirring often, until caramelised. This should take about 5 minutes.
3. Add the red wine, chicken stock, carrot, leek, celery and tortellini and simmer for approx. 6 minutes or until the tortellini are al dente.
4. Ladle the soup into bowls and garnish with the Parmesan cheese and fresh herbs.

Seafood bouillon with alfabetini

1 tbsp olive oil
1 onion, minced
3 cloves garlic, minced
1 celery stalk, cut into small segments
1 carrot, cut into small chunks
1 leek, cut into half-circles
handful of fresh parsley, minced
0.5l (2 cups) fish stock
0.5l (2 cups) dry white wine
200g (7oz) alfabetini (alphabet noodles)
250g (9oz) fish filets (tilapia or any other firm white fish), in good-sized chunks.
200g (7oz) shrimp, boiled
200g (7oz) mussels, boiled

1. Heat the oil in a pan and sauté the onion and garlic for 1 minute. Add the vegetables and parsley and cook for another minute, stirring constantly.
2. Pour in the wine and the stock. Bring to the boil, then stir in the pasta. Reduce the heat to a low simmer and heat a further 5 minutes to let the flavours combine.
3. Stir in the fish filets and cook for approx. 5 minutes. Add the mussels and shrimp and heat through well.
4. Make sure the pasta is tender and serve the soup in shallow bowls.

Minestrone with porcini mushrooms and chicken filets

100g (3.5oz) dried porcini mushrooms, soaked for 1 hour in lukewarm water
1l (4 cups) chicken stock
200g (7oz) pipe rigate
2 carrots, thinly sliced
2 chicken filets, cut into small chunks
200g (7oz) haricots verts
baguette, for serving

1. Strain the porcini through a sieve, pressing out as much of the liquid as possible. Reserve the liquid.
2. Bring the porcini liquid and the chicken stock to a boil and add the pipe rigate. Bring to the boil again, then reduce the heat to a simmer.
3. After approx. 5 minutes, add the carrot slices and the haricots.
4. Cook for a further 2 minutes, then add the pieces of chicken and simmer until the chicken is cooked and the pasta is al dente.
5. Portion the soup into shallow bowls and serve with baguette slices.

Sweet in flavour, always available, and cheap. Where would we be without carrots? Much of the root's sweetness is directly underneath the peel, so gently scrape them clean or use a thin-bladed peeler which does not remove too much.

Dried porcini mushrooms (funghi porcini) are a staple of Italian cuisine. These have a pungent, concentrated aroma and flavour; a little will go a long way.

Ⓥ Cabbage soup with pesto

2 tbsp olive oil

1 leek, cut into rings

2 cloves of garlic, pressed

2 potatoes, peeled and diced

1l (4 cups) vegetable stock

100g (3.5oz) gramigna

1 small pointed or spring cabbage, sliced

3 tbsp pesto (see recipe on page 82)

toasted baguette slices for serving

1. Heat the oil in a large pan and add the leek, garlic and diced potato. Stirring constantly, sauté for about 1 minute. Do not allow the mixture to deepen in colour.
2. Pour in the stock and bring to the boil. Add the pasta and reduce the heat. Simmer on low heat for a few minutes.
3. Stir the cabbage and pesto into the soup and cook for another minute or until the pasta is al dente.
4. Serve with toasted baguette slices.

This recipe calls for a special kind of cabbage. Known as pointed, spring, or sometimes oxheart cabbage (you will occasionally find it under its Dutch name, 'spitskool'), it is milder and more delicate than the usual white or red cabbage, making it a nice addition to salads. Remove the harder outer leaves and the stalk. Wash the cabbage and slice it into strips.

Ⓥ Roasted vegetable soup with pipe rigate

500g (18oz) tomatoes, halved
1 sweet red pepper, cut into large pieces
1 large red onion, cut into large pieces
1 red chilli pepper, halved lengthwise and
seeded
half a carrot
2 cloves of garlic, peeled
1 tbsp olive oil
1l (4 cups) vegetable stock
100g (3.5oz) pipe rigate
small handful of basil, finely chopped

1. Preheat the oven to 200°C (400° F or gas mark 6).
2. Lay the tomatoes, pepper, red onion, chilli pepper, carrot and garlic in a single layer in a casserole dish and drizzle with the oil. Roast the vegetables for 30 minutes in the oven, turning them over after 15 minutes.
3. Remove the vegetables and puree them in a food processor or with a hand-held blender. Strain the puree through a sieve, stirring constantly.
4. Pour the stock into a pot, stir in the roasted vegetable mixture and bring to a boil.
5. Add the pipe rigate and simmer on low heat until al dente.
6. Stir in the basil immediately before serving. Serve warm.

Chicken soup with capelli d'angelo

1l (4 cups) chicken stock
1 onion, chopped
1 leek, white part only, cut into half-circles
small handful of celery leaves, finely chopped
100g (3.5oz) capelli d'angelo ('angel hair')
200g (7oz) cooked chicken, in small chunks

1. Bring the stock to the boil and add the onion, leek, celery leaves and pasta. Simmer on low heat for several minutes, stirring occasionally.
2. Stir in the meat and serve the soup in small bowls.

The leek (allum porrum) belongs to the same family as onion and garlic (elephant garlic, in fact, is actually a kind of leek) and is available in a number of varieties, depending on the season. Summer leeks have a finer structure than autumn or winter leeks and are lighter in colour. Leek growers try to cultivate their crop as deep in the soil as possible, ensuring that the tender white portion (the edible part) grows longest.

Mushroom soup with conchiglie rigate

(V)

1l (4 cups) vegetable or mushroom stock
100ml (3.5oz) dry sherry
250g (9oz) mixed mushrooms of your choice (crimini,
porcini, cantharelles, etc.), brushed clean
200g (7oz) conchiglie rigate
small handful of fresh parsley, minced
toasted baguette slices for serving

1. Bring the stock to the boil and pour in the sherry.
2. While the stock is heating, de-stem the mushrooms.
3. Stir the mushroom stems into the bouillon and simmer on low heat for about 5 minutes.
4. Strain the soup and return to the boil.
5. Cook the conchiglie rigate until al dente in the soup.
6. Add the mushroom caps and parsley a few minutes before the pasta is done.
7. Pour the soup into shallow bowls and serve with toasted baguette slices.

Fresh mushrooms can be kept a few days at most in the vegetable drawer of your refrigerator. Separate them with dry tea towels or paper towels. Never store mushrooms in plastic; they need ventilation to keep from spoiling.

Fresh herbs

Herbs flourish all over Italy: growing wild, in gardens or in window boxes. Their unique aromas, flavours and colours liven up any dish. And what would pasta be without fresh herbs?

Parsley (prezzemolo)

Fresh parsley is an indispensable component of many pasta dishes. The freshly minced leaves are often sprinkled on top directly before serving to lend the dish a little colour and a fresh flavour. The stems need not go to waste either; add them to the sauce for some extra flavour. Whenever an Italian recipe calls for parsley, this usually means the flat-leaf variety, which has a more pungent flavour and a thicker texture than the curly variety.

Bay (alloro)

These aromatic leaves can often be found simmering away in the saucepan whenever a slow-cooked sauce is needed. Bay, or laurel, *offers a refined counterbalance to meaty blends* like ragù alla Bolognese and is most potent when fresh. Italian gardens often have a grove of bay trees, ensuring that there's always some on hand. If you can't find fresh bay leaves, the dried work fine too.

Rosemary (rosmarino)

This savoury herb is most often used in meat dishes and roasts. It appears less in pasta sauces. Sprigs of rosemary are sometimes simmered in stews and removed before serving, like bay. Tender young leaves can be finely chopped and added to tomato or herb sauces.

Sage (salvia)

Burro e salvia is a classic, super-quick and tasty sauce for serving with gnocchi and ricotta-stuffed ravioli, among other things. The sauce consists of nothing more than hot melted butter infused with sage leaves.

Oregano (origano)

Oregano is more or less the only herb which is used in dried form as often as fresh. It is a popular seasoning for pizza, in pasta sauces with roasted vegetables and – fresh or dried – in a wide variety of tomato sauces.

Rocket (rucola)

Rocket's deliciously piquant and nutty-tasting leaves must be used raw, as they will quickly lose their flavour when cooked. They are often used to make pesto, as a substitute for basil.

Basil (basilico)

Cooking Italian food without basil is almost inconceivable. The herb is famous, of course, as the main ingredient in pesto alla Genovese, it also plays a role in thousands of pasta dishes. Like parsley, it is usually sprinkled over a dish right before serving, though it can also be very briefly cooked with the other ingredients.

Pasta alle erbe

Sauté an onion and a little garlic in a lump of butter and throw in a small handful of each of the herbs listed above, all finely chopped (except the bay: add one whole leaf instead). Briefly cook the herbs in the onion mixture, then pour in a generous dash of white wine. Let simmer for a couple minutes, then add a dash of stock and continue to cook. Remove and discard the bay leaf. Toss the sauce with fresh egg pasta.

Do the Italians really have a more diverse diet than us? You'd be surprised. The biggest difference is that in Italy, pasta is served as a separate course, before the main dish. The cook concentrates on using simple ingredients to make a tasty pasta dish which can stand on its own as a single course. This is why there are so many wonderful vegetarian pasta creations that are actually quite easy to prepare.

Pasta with vegetables & fresh herbs

The meat usually comes afterwards, as the main course. It is never the intention to use a lot of expensive ingredients to make a day-to-day meal – an easy fresh tomato and herb sauce, some choice vegetables sautéed in olive oil, a handful of nice cheese or olives and you already have a very tasty primo. Pasta is so nourishing and delectable – even without meat or fish – that it is very popular as a modern vegetarian main course. One important rule of thumb: the fewer ingredients you use, the better quality they have to be. Spend the time you save on cooking on doing your grocery shopping and keep your eyes out for rich, ripe plum tomatoes, fresh (preferably organic) vegetables, well-aged cheese to grate at home, and, of course, good olive oil.

ⓥ Lasagnette with pomodorini and garlic

1 pint of pomodorini (cherry tomatoes), halved
16 cloves of garlic, halved
8 tbsp olive oil
salt and pepper
400g (14oz) lasagnette

1. Preheat the oven to 180 °C (350° F or gas mark 4).
2. Put the tomatoes and garlic in a casserole dish. Pour the olive oil over the top and sprinkle with salt and pepper. Bake for approx. 25 minutes.
3. When the tomatoes and garlic are almost done, cook the lasagnette until al dente in a large pot of boiling salted water.
4. Strain the lasagnette and toss them with the tomato, garlic and the juice left in the casserole dish. Divide over 4 deep plates and serve immediately.

ⓥ Tagliatelle with parsley-lemon oil

400g (14oz) tagliatelle
salt
small handful of parsley, minced
zest + juice of one lemon
4 tbsp olive oil
sea salt and black pepper
4 tbsp pine nuts, toasted in a dry pan on very low heat

1. Cook the tagliatelle until al dente in a large pot of boiling salted water.
2. While the pasta cooks, use an hand-held blender to puree the parsley and lemon zest together with the lemon juice and olive oil. Add sea salt and black pepper to taste.
3. Strain the tagliatelle and toss with the parsley-lemon oil and pine nuts.
4. Portion onto plates and serve immediately.

When roasted in the oven, garlic becomes velvety soft, surprisingly sweet, and eminently spreadable. Bake a whole bulb for half an hour on medium heat. Remove from the oven and cut the bulb in half through the middle. Open it up and pick out the garlic paste with a butter knife to spread on bruschetta, etc.

Fusilli tricolore with zucchini flowers

200ml (7oz) vegetable bouillon
100ml (3.5oz) dry white wine
200ml (7oz) single cream
100g (3.5oz) sun-dried tomatoes, thinly sliced
6 small courgettes with the flowers still on
1 tbsp olive oil
1 clove garlic, minced
400g (14oz) fusilli tricolore (Grand'Italia)

1. Simmer the vegetable stock, wine and cream down to half the original amount, adding the sun-dried tomatoes for the last 2 minutes.
2. Puree the sauce with a hand-held blender.
3. Cut the courgette flowers into large strips and the courgettes into thin strips.
4. Heat the oil in a pan and sauté the garlic and courgettes until tender. Add this to the sauce, then gently stir in the flowers. Save a few flowers for garnishing
5. Cook the pasta until al dente in a large pot of boiling salted water. Strain and mix into the sauce.
6. Portion onto plates and garnish with the flowers. Serve immediately.

ⓥ Spaghetti with olives, tomatoes and rocket

400g (14oz) spaghetti

salt

50g (1.75oz) green olives, pitted

50g (1.75oz) black olives, pitted

4 tomatoes, each cut into 6 pieces

small handful of fresh oregano, finely chopped

small handful fresh basil, finely chopped

50g (1.75oz) rocket, coarsely chopped

2 tbsp balsamic vinegar

2 tbsp olive oil

sea salt and freshly ground black pepper

1. Cook the spaghetti until al dente in a large pot of boiling salted water.
2. While the pasta cooks, mix the olives, tomato, oregano, basil and rocket. Drizzle with the olive oil and balsamic vinegar and sprinkle with sea salt and freshly ground black pepper.
3. Strain the spaghetti and portion onto plates. Top with the olive mixture and serve lukewarm.

ⓥ Spaghetti with fresh tomato sauce

1 tbsp olive oil

1 large onion, minced

1 clove of garlic, minced

1 carrot, cut into small chunks

1 celery stalk, cut into small segments

small handful of parsley plus extra

for garnishing, finely chopped

2 tbsp tomato puree

500g (18oz) ripe tomatoes, seeded and diced,

plus a few slices for garnishing

salt and pepper

400g (14oz) spaghetti

50g (1.75oz) Parmesan cheese, cut very thin

with a cheese slicer

1. Heat the oil in a pan and sauté the onion and garlic until translucent. Add the chunks of carrot, the pieces of celery and the finely chopped parsley and sauté 1 minute longer.
2. Stir the tomato puree and diced tomato into the vegetable mixture and cook for 5 minutes. Add salt and pepper to taste, reduce the heat and simmer on low for 30 minutes, stirring occasionally.
3. When the sauce is almost done, cook the spaghetti until al dente in a large pot of boiling salted water.
4. Strain the pasta, portion into deep plates and top with the fresh tomato sauce. Garnish with tomato slices and sprinkle with grated Parmesan cheese and parsley. Serve immediately.

Parsley is a diuretic, stimulates the blood circulation and contains a large amount of vitamin C.

Rucola, or 'rocket', is worthy of the name – the plant shoots up incredibly fast. Rucola has been cultivated in Mediterranean countries for centuries. Good rocket has long, aromatic leaves of a peppery and slightly bitter flavour. People seem either to love it or hate it!

Tagliatelle with artichoke hearts and capers

400g (14oz) tagliatelle
salt
1 courgette, cut into small chunks
1 tbsp olive oil
1 onion, chopped
2 cloves of garlic, minced
100ml (3.5oz) vegetable stock
small handful of minced chives
small handful of parsley, finely chopped
small handful of fresh oregano, finely chopped
1 can of artichoke hearts (400g or 14oz), quartered
1 tbsp capers
75g (2.5oz) Parmesan cheese,
cut very thin with a cheese slicer

1. Cook the tagliatelle until al dente in a large pot of boiling salted water.
2. While the pasta cooks, boil the pieces of courgette for about 2 minutes in a separate pot. Remove from the pot and puree with an hand-held blender.
3. Heat the oil in a pan and sauté the onion and garlic until translucent. Add the courgette puree, the vegetable stock, chives, parsley and oregano and stir well. Mix in the artichoke hearts and capers.
4. Strain the tagliatelle and portion into bowls or onto plates. Ladle the artichoke sauce over the top and garnish with Parmesan cheese. Serve immediately.

Artichokes belong to the thistle family and are cultivated for their edible buds. Carciofi alla Romana is a well-known *Italian artichoke dish*. Fresh artichokes are stuffed with a mixture of garlic, mint leaves, olive oil and bread crumbs, then roasted in the oven.

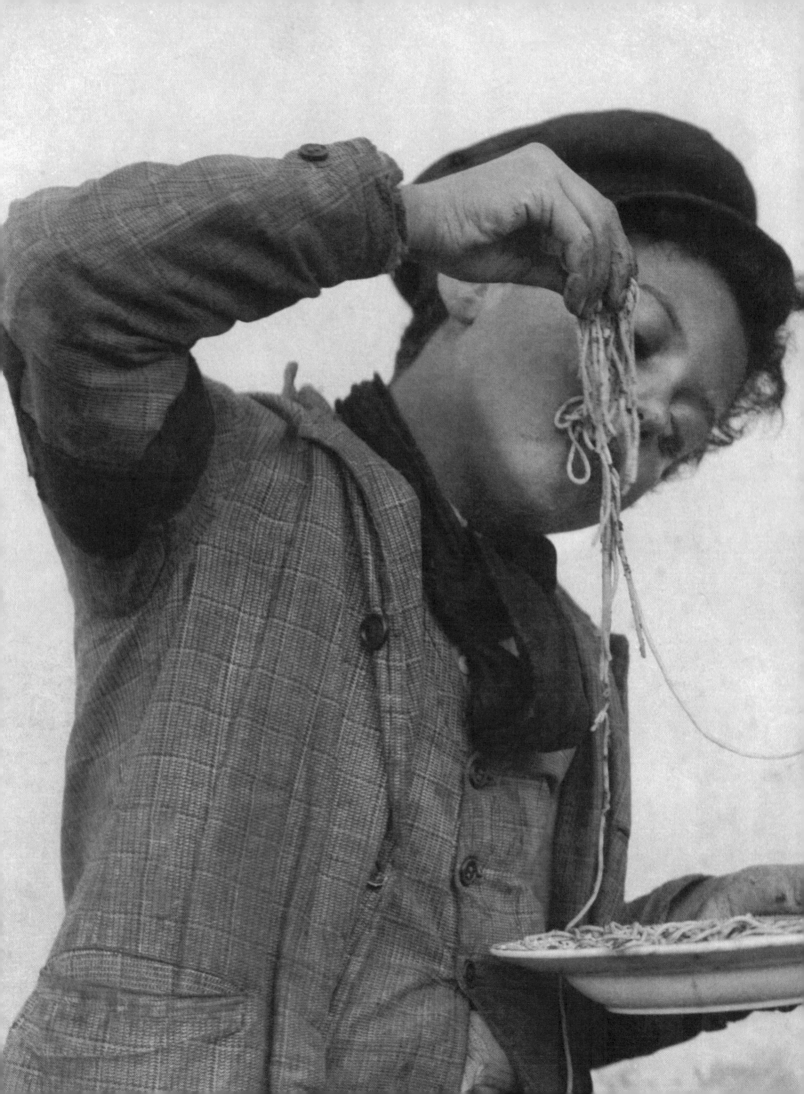

Mushroom lasagne

(V)

1. Preheat the oven to 180°C (350°F or gas mark 4).
2. Melt the butter for the béchamel sauce in a pan until it starts to foam. Add the flour and whisk well. Continue whisking until the mixture (now roux) is a smooth consistency; this takes several minutes. The roux should not stick or solidify and only slightly deepen in colour.
3. Remove the pan from the heat and pour in the warm milk a little at a time. Continue stirring well to prevent lumps. Return the pan to the heat and add salt, pepper and a pinch of nutmeg to taste. Keep the sauce on the heat, stirring constantly, for another 5 minutes or so. Remove from the heat and set aside for later.
4. Heat the oil in a frying pan and sauté the mushrooms and onion on high heat, stirring every few minutes. Add the garlic and sauté another minute.
5. Stir the cream, eggs, parsley and half of the béchamel sauce into the mushroom mixture and add salt and pepper to taste.
6. Coat the bottom of a greased casserole dish with a layer of mushroom sauce. Cover with a layer of lasagna sheets, then more sauce and continue in this order until the dish is filled, ending with the mushroom sauce. Pour the remaining béchamel sauce over the top and sprinkle with the Parmesan cheese. Bake the lasagne for approximately 30 minutes or until golden brown.

1 tbsp olive oil + extra for greasing
100g (3.5oz) shiitakes
200g (7oz) white button mushrooms, sliced
100g (3.5oz) chestnut mushrooms, sliced
100g (3.5oz) oyster mushrooms,
torn into medium-sized pieces
1 onion, chopped
1 clove of garlic, minced
100ml (3.5oz) single cream
2 eggs, beaten
small handful of parsley, minced
salt and pepper
1 package lasagna pasta (500g or 18oz),
pre-cooked if necessary (most brands do not
require pre-cooking)
100g (3.5oz) Parmesan cheese, grated

For the béchamel sauce:
60g (2oz) butter
60g (2oz) wheat flour
1l (4 cups) milk, warm
salt and pepper
pinch of ground nutmeg

The two most common parsley varieties are curly-leaf parsley and flat-leaf, or Italian, parsley. The latter has a higher moisture content and contains more essential oils, which give it a more refined flavour.

ⓥ Pappardelle with sun-dried tomatoes and pine nuts

400g (14oz) pappardelle

salt

2 tbsp olive oil

2 cloves of garlic, minced

4 tbsp sun-dried tomatoes in oil, cut into strips

1 can of artichoke hearts (400g or 14oz), halved

handful of fresh basil, chopped

100g (3.5oz) Parmesan cheese, grated

2 tbsp pine nuts, toasted in a dry pan on very low heat

freshly grated pepper

1. Cook the pappardelle until al dente in a large pot of boiling salted water.
2. While the pasta cooks, heat the oil in a large pan and sauté the garlic. Add the sun-dried tomatoes and continue cooking for another minute, stirring constantly.
3. Strain the pappardelle and mix it into the sun-dried tomatoes. Toss with the artichoke hearts, basil, Parmesan cheese and pine nuts. Add salt and pepper to taste.
4. Portion onto plates or into bowls and serve immediately.

ⓥ Perciatelli with spicy tomato sauce

1 can peeled Italian tomatoes (400g or 14oz)

3 tbsp olive oil

1 onion, minced

1 carrot, finely chopped

1 celery stalk, finely chopped

2 cloves garlic, peeled

1 red chilli pepper, minced, with or

without the seeds (depending on the desired heat)

2 tbsp chopped fresh garden herbs (basil, parsley, oregano and thyme)

salt and pepper

400g (14oz) perciatelli

1. Cut the tomatoes into large chunks and drain the excess juice.
2. Heat the oil in a large pan and sauté the onion, carrot and celery until the onion is translucent. Add the peeled garlic and chilli pepper and cook for another minute.
3. Stir the tomatoes and herbs into the vegetable mixture and add salt and pepper to taste. Simmer gently on low heat for approx. 20 minutes, stirring occasionally.
4. When the sauce is almost done, cook the perciatelle until al dente in a large pot of boiling salted water.
5. Strain the tomato sauce through a sieve, drain the pasta and toss with the sauce.
6. Portion into bowls and serve immediately.

It happens to everyone sooner or later: you casually rub your eyes, forgetting that you just cut up a handful of chilli peppers. You can avoid this unpleasantness with a little preventative trick: simply rub your hands with olive oil before touching any chillis. Of course, putting a plastic bag over them works too.

Pine nuts have the highest protein content of any nut or seed, with 31 grams of protein for every 100 grams of nuts.

Paglia e fieno with red pesto

400g (14oz) Paglia e fieno (Grand'Italia)
75g (2.5oz) pine nuts,
toasted in a dry frying pan
150g (5oz) sun-dried tomatoes
4 tbsp olive oil

1. Cook the pasta until al dente in a large pot of boiling salted water.

2. For the red pesto, puree the pine nuts and sun-dried tomatoes in a food processor or crush with a mortar and pestle. Add the olive oil at the end and mix well.

3. Carefully toss the pesto into the pasta and divide over 4 plates. Serve immediately.

No food processor or mortar and pestle? If you want to make it really easy for yourself, go for a good quality ready-to-eat red pesto (Grand'Italia). Stir it right into the al dente pasta e presto… buon appetito!

ⓥ Farfalle with green sauce

400g (14oz) farfalle (Grand'Italia)
salt
100ml (3.5oz) vegetable stock
100g (3.5oz) haricots verts, rinsed and cut into small segments
100g (3.5oz) snow peas (mange touts), cut into small segments
1 red chilli pepper, seeded and cut into thin strips
freshly grated pepper
handful of parsley, chopped
handful of basil, chopped

1. Cook the farfalle until al dente in a large pot of boiling salted water.
2. While the pasta cooks, pour the stock into a large pan and bring to a boil. Add the haricots, snow peas and chilli pepper, reduce the heat and simmer for a few minutes or until the vegetables are just tender. Add salt and pepper to taste.
3. Strain the farfalle. Stir the herbs into the green sauce. Toss the pasta with the sauce.
4. Portion onto plates or into bowls and serve immediately.

ⓥ Macaroni with aubergine and mozzarella

2 tbsp olive oil
1 clove garlic, coarsely chopped
2 aubergines, cut into small cubes
4 tomatoes, seeded and diced
small handful of basil, coarsely chopped
400g (14oz) macaroni (Grand'Italia)
salt
2 mozzarella balls, cut into small cubes

1. Heat the olive oil in a large pan and sauté the garlic for about 1 minute on low heat. Add the cubes of aubergine and sauté another 5 minutes or so on medium heat, stirring constantly to prevent sticking.
2. Stir in the tomato and basil.
3. Cook the macaroni until al dente in a large pot of boiling salted water.
4. Strain the pasta and portion it over 4 plates. Stir the mozzarella cubes into the aubergine mixture and scoop over the pasta. Serve immediately.

Although in these modern times you can find fresh haricots verts all year round, the domestic growing season for northern Europe runs from late July to September. From March to October the greenhouse varieties are available and from October to June stores offer imports from Kenya, Egypt, Spain and Italy.

Botanically speaking, the aubergine is a fruit, not a vegetable. There are countless varieties of aubergines, the one overarching quality being a comparatively mild, slightly smoky flavour and a sponge-like texture when raw, which becomes velvety soft when cooked. Always go for firm, shiny and heavy-feeling aubergines.

Tagliatelle with spring vegetables

(V)

400g (14oz) green tagliatelle
salt
3 tbsp olive oil
1 onion, minced
1 clove of garlic, minced
1 sweet red pepper, diced
250g (9oz) snow peas (mange touts), blanched (submerge
in boiling water for 2-3 minutes, remove and rinse under
cold water)
1 small courgette, cut into half-circles
125g (4.5oz) button mushrooms, sliced
small handful of parsley, chopped
2 drops of tabasco sauce
2 tbsp pine nuts, toasted in a dry pan on very low heat

1. Cook the tagliatelle until al dente in a large pot of boiling salted water.
2. While the pasta cooks, heat the olive oil in a large deep pan and briefly sauté the onion and garlic. Add the pepper and snow peas and sauté another minute.
3. Stir the courgette, the mushrooms, parsley and tabasco into the vegetable mixture and simmer another minute on low heat.
4. Strain the tagliatelle and mix into the vegetables. Heat through well and portion onto plates. Sprinkle with the pine nuts and serve immediately.

Pasta primavera is not a traditional Italian recipe but an Italian-American invention of the 1970s. Though there had been a dish called Lasagne primavera in Italy, the now-famous pasta and spring vegetable dish was the brainchild of Sirio Maccioni, a celebrity restaurateur in New York City. The recipe created a sensation among Manhattan gourmets. And, as we all know, they are the hardest people to please!

Italian meats & dried sausages

Each region of Italy has its own meat specialities. When making traditional recipes, always try to find the original ham, bacon or sausage type. You will definitely taste the difference! These are the most famous:

Pancetta

Pancetta, a bit like breakfast bacon, is a pork belly cut. The name usually refers to the roll-up variety *(pancetta arrotolata)*, which gives you round slices. It is salted but not smoked. Smoked pancetta (pancetta affumicata) is not rolled, and the slices are oblong rather than round. Paper-thin slices of pancetta make a great antipasto. If using it in a pasta sauce (carbonara, for instance), ask the butcher to make the slices thicker than normal, so they can be cut into nice cubes or strips.

Lardo and speck

You don't need to speak much Italian to figure out what lardo means – this is bacon without the meat, i.e. only the fat. *Speck from South Tirol is similar to bacon:* it is salted, smoked, then dried.

Salami

This salted, dried pork sausage is made in all parts of Italy. It is frequently seasoned with garlic, as is the case with salame Milano, and is often diversified with all sorts of other seasonings as well. *Tuscan salame Fiorentina, or* Florentine salami, is made with fennel seed and pepper, while salame di Felino, from the area around Parma, has garlic and white wine, and salame Sardo contains spicy red peppers.

Parma ham

Specially selected Italian pigs are lovingly raised on a diet of grain and whey, the liquid remaining after production of Parmesan cheese. Only the meat of the animals' heavy hind legs are used. The 'salt master' rubs the ham with sea salt before it's hung up to cure in rooms with large windows, allowing the fresh Parma air to make its mark on the meat. The pork cures for at least one year before being given its 'crown', the stamp of true prosciutto *di Parma*.

San Daniele

Even more exclusive than parma ham is the prosciutto *crudo (dried ham) produced in the town of San Daniele* in Lombardy. The pigs are kept outside and fed on acorns, giving their meat a distinctive flavour.

Bresaola

This Alpine specialty consists of dried and salted beef. The best varieties are made from the tenderloin cut.

The romantic image we have of Italy — namely that people still grow their own food, make everything fresh and even butcher their own meat — still applies in many villages. Chickens and geese flock across the farmyards, providing eggs for egg pasta and meat for the ragù. There is still a law, for example, allowing Umbrians to raise pigs and slaughter them for their meat. There are many people who do this, and every part of the animal is used. Each region of the country has its own specialties: the famous parma ham and other prosciutto *crudo (dried ham), pancetta (bacon,* smoked or not), coppa (dried and salted ham cut from the less delectable parts of the animal) and all sorts of salami. The quantity of meat which goes into a pasta sauce is generally kept quite modest; it is a seasoning meant to enhance the pasta,

Pasta with meat & poultry

not to be served as the dish's main component. Meat is usually minced or cut into small pieces, allowing it to stick to the pasta better. The best-known meat sauce for pasta is ragù, actually a generalised term for any slow-cooked sauce made with mincemeat and tomato. Practically every region has its own variant, including, of course, Bologna. 'Bolognese sauce' is made with a mixture of beef and pork, though similar ragùs are made with mutton in the south and with game in Tuscany. Larger pieces of meat go best with short or broad pasta, any variety which will keep them from slipping off. In some modern pasta recipes, slices of meat are also served on a bed of pasta and sauce, especially if eaten as the main course.

Green tagliatelle with chicken filets in white wine sauce

2 tbsp olive oil

2 chicken filets, cut into small chunks

salt and pepper

1 small courgette, cut into small chunks

small handful of fresh thyme, finely chopped (plus half a tablespoon coarsely chopped for garnishing)

small handful of basil, finely chopped

100ml (3.5oz) chicken stock

100ml (3.5oz) dry white wine

200ml (7oz) cooking cream

400g (14oz) tagliatelle verdi all 'uovo (Grand'Italia)

1. Heat the oil in a large pan and fry the pieces of chicken until brown on each side. Sprinkle with salt and pepper.

2. Add the courgette, thyme and basil to the chicken and sauté another minute, stirring constantly. Remove from the pan.

3. Pour the chicken stock, wine and cream into the empty pan. Mix well and bring to a boil. Reduce the heat and simmer on low for 15 minutes.

4. Cook the tagliatelle until al dente in a large pot of boiling salted water.

5. Stir the chicken and courgette mixture into the white wine sauce and add salt and pepper to taste.

6. Strain the tagliatelle and mix it directly into the sauce. Portion onto four plates, sprinkle with the coarsely chopped thyme and serve.

The smaller the courgette, the more flavour it has. Large courgettes are often hydroponically grown, giving them less flavour than their earth-grown counterparts. Always go for a truffle oil infused with real truffles and truffle shavings, rather than synthetic truffle essence. You only need a few drops of good truffle oil for an intense flavour. Always keep this delicate oil in a cool, dry spot in order to retain its flavour.

Pipe rigate with stewed beef and San Daniele

2 tbsp olive oil

1 onion, minced

100g (3.5oz) San Daniele (or parma ham), cut into strips

500g (18oz) stewing beef, cubed

salt and pepper

generous handful of fresh parsley, minced

half a carrot, sliced

1 celery stalk, thinly sliced

200ml (7oz) red wine

4 tomatoes, seeded and diced

beef bouillon(optional)

400g (14oz) pipe rigate

1. Heat 1 tbsp oil in a pan and sauté the onion and San Daniele on medium heat until the onion is translucent.
2. Heat the remaining oil in another large pan and fry the stewing meat until brown on each side. Sprinkle with salt and pepper.
3. Add the onion and San Daniele, parsley, carrot and celery to the meat, then the red wine and pieces of tomato. Stew, covered, until all the moisture has evaporated and the meat is cooked (this takes about 1 hour). If it looks like it's getting too dry, pour in a little beef bouillon.
4. Cook the pipe rigate until al dente in a large pot of boiling salted water.
5. Strain the pasta and toss with the meat mixture. Serve immediately.

Tagliatelle with tenderloin and truffle sauce

400 g tagliatelle

salt

2 tbsp olive oil

1 small pointed or spring cabbage, thinly sliced.

1 tbsp butter

400g (14oz) tenderloin, in strips

100g (3.5oz) shiitake mushrooms

pepper

For the truffle sauce:

4 tbsp milk

1 tbsp truffle oil

2 tbsp pecorino, grated

1. First make the truffle sauce. Warm the milk in a small pan, remove from the heat and whisk in the truffle oil and grated pecorino.
2. Cook the tagliatelle until al dente in a large pot of boiling salted water.
3. While the pasta cooks, heat 1 tbsp of oil in a wok or large pan and stir-fry the cabbage slices for about 1 minute. Stir in the truffle sauce and remove from the heat.
4. Strain the tagliatelle and mix into the cabbage and truffle sauce.
5. Heat the remaining oil with the butter in a pan on high heat. Sauté the strips of tenderloin for about 1 minute or until brown on each side. Add the shiitakes and cook for another minute on high heat. Sprinkle with salt and pepper.
6. Portion the pasta onto plates and top with the tenderloin.

Always choose truffle oil that has been made from real truffles or truffle skins instead of synthetic truffle essence. You only need a little of the real truffle oil for an intense truffle taste. Keep the delicate oil in a cool, dark place.

Tortelloni prosciutto crudo in creamy tomato sauce

100 ml (3.5 oz) dry white wine
150 ml (5 oz) panna or cooking cream
6 ripe tomatoes, peeled and cut into chunks
100 g (3.5 oz) prosciutto crudo (such as parma ham), cut into strips
400 g (14 oz) tortelloni prosciutto crudo (Grand'Italia)
small handful of rocket, coarsely chopped
freshly ground black pepper

1. Heat the wine and cream in a pan, add the tomatoes and simmer for 5 minutes. Puree with a hand-held blender.
2. Cook the tortelloni, following the directions on the package. Strain.
3. Stir the strips of ham into the sauce, followed by the tortelloni.
4. Top with the rocket and sprinkle with pepper before serving.

Mafaldine with salame cacciatore

400g mafaldine or lasagnette
2 tbsp olive oil
1 salami (or other spicy dried sausage), in chunks
2 cloves of garlic, thinly sliced

1. Cook the mafaldine until al dente in a large pot of boiling salted water.
2. While the pasta cooks, heat the oil in a large pan and sauté the slices of garlic on low heat until golden brown. Add the sausage and keep on low heat for another minute.
3. Strain the mafaldine and mix into the garlic and sausage mixture.
4. Divide the pasta over 4 bowls and serve immediately.

The word mafaldine was coined in honour of Mafalde of Savoy, second daughter of King Emanuele III of Italy and Elena of Spain.

Maccheroncine with chicken filets in mushroom sauce

2 tbsp olive oil
1 clove of garlic, minced
400g (14oz) chicken filets, in strips
400g (14oz) mixed mushrooms of your choice (oyster mushrooms, cantharelles, brown button mushrooms, etc.)
400g (14oz) maccheroncini
salt

For the sauce:
100ml (3.5oz) vegetable stock
100ml (3.5oz) dry white wine
100ml (3.5oz) cooking cream
2 tbsp truffle oil

1. Mix the ingredients for the sauce in a small pan and bring to a boil. Turn down the flame and simmer gently for 10 minutes.
2. When the sauce is almost done, cook the maccheroncini until al dente in a large pot of boiling salted water.
3. While the pasta cooks, heat 1 tablespoon of oil in a pan and sauté the garlic for 1 minute on low heat. Put on high heat, throw in the strips of chicken and cook for approx. 2 minutes or until brown on each side.
4. Meanwhile, place the mushrooms in a separate pan on high heat (without oil) until the juice has been released and cooks off. Then add one tablespoon of oil and sauté the mushrooms for another minute, stirring constantly. Add the sauce to the pan and stir well.
5. Strain the maccheroncini and immediately portion into deep plates. Top with the chicken and pour the mushroom sauce over both the meat and the pasta. Serve immediately.

Do not keep brown button mushrooms near citrus. Citrus fruit releases a compound which makes them spoil faster. It's also a good idea not to store them near strong-smelling vegetables like leeks or onions, as mushrooms easily absorb other aromas.

Pasta is sometimes called 'the world's most democratic dish' because everyone can enjoy it equally. It is a boon for those who don't have a lot of money to spend because the ingredients (wheat and water) are so cheap. Those who do have money, however, enjoy it as well – just with a generous drizzle of truffle sauce or other luxurious additions!

Whole-grain penne with sausage and roasted garlic

16 cloves of garlic, peeled
olive oil
200ml (7oz) meatstock
200ml (7oz) single cream
100ml (3.5oz) red wine
200g (7oz) Italian pork sausage,
cut into small chunks
400g (14oz) penne rigate integrali (Grand'Italia)
50g (1.75oz) pecorino, grated

1. Preheat the oven to 200°C (400°F or gas mark 6).
2. Roast the garlic: place the 16 cloves in a casserole dish and pour olive oil over them until they are completely covered. Bake for approx. 15 minutes or until they are soft all the way through. They should float to the top when done.
4. In a small pot, cook the stock, cream and red wine down to half the original quantity. Stir in half the garlic cloves and puree with an hand-held blender.
5. Heat 1 tablespoon of olive oil in a pan and fry the sausage for several minutes, until cooked.
6. Cook the pasta until al dente in a large pot of boiling salted water. Strain and toss with the sausage and sauce. Top with the cheese and remaining garlic cloves. Serve immediately.

This recipe does not call for any further use of the oil left after roasting the garlic. But, of course, just tossing it out would be a sin! Hold on to this tasty, garlic-infused oil for making spaghetti aglio e olio for use in anything from roasted meat or potatoes to salad dressings!

Fettuccelle with pork tenderloin in creamy mushroom sauce

1 tbsp olive oil
500g (18oz) pork tenderloin
salt and pepper
400g (14oz) fettuccelle

For the sauce:
1 onion, minced
1 clove garlic, minced
250g (9oz) mushrooms
100ml (3.5oz) dry sherry
100ml (3.5oz) beef bouillon
100ml (3.5oz) cooking cream
small handful of parsley, minced

1. Preheat the oven to 160°C (325°F or gas mark 3).
2. Heat the oil in a large pan and briefly sauté the pork until brown on each side. Sprinkle with salt and pepper and place in a casserole dish. Bake for 20 minutes.
3. When the meat is almost done, cook the fettuccelle until al dente in a large pot of boiling salted water.
4. Meanwhile, return the pan used for the pork to the heat and sauté the onion and garlic until translucent. Add the mushrooms and continue sautéing for one minute, stirring constantly. Pour in the sherry, the bouillon and the single cream and bring to a boil. Reduce the heat and simmer gently for about 5 minutes. Stir in the parsley and continue cooking for one more minute.
5. Take the meat out of the oven and slice it. Cover with aluminium foil to keep it warm.
6. Strain the fettuccelle and portion onto plates. Ladle the mushroom sauce over the pasta and top with the pork tenderloin. Serve right away.

The potency of any bulb of garlic depends on the variety as well its freshness. Always remove the green shoot from the centre of the peeled clove if there is one, because this new growth will taste unpleasantly bitter when heated.

Fusilli with minced lamb and mustard

1 tbsp olive oil
400g (14oz) minced lamb
1 onion, finely chopped
500g (18oz) vine tomatoes, seeded and diced
200ml (7oz) red wine
2 tbsp mustard
small handful of basil, finely chopped
salt and pepper
400g (14oz) fusilli (Grand'Italia)
100g (3.5oz) pecorino, grated

1. Heat the olive oil in a pan and sauté the minced lamb, stirring to keep it loose. Add the onion and continue cooking, stirring constantly, until the onion is translucent and the meat brown.
2. Stir in the tomatoes, the wine, mustard and basil and mix well. Simmer on low heat for 5 minutes and add salt and pepper to taste.
3. Meanwhile, cook the fusilli until al dente in a large pot of boiling salted water.
4. Strain the fusilli and mix into the lamb sauce.
5. Portion into deep plates or bowls and serve the pecorino on the side.

Pipe rigate with parma ham and green peas

1 tbsp olive oil
1 onion, minced
300g (10.5oz) green peas (fresh or frozen)
100ml (3.5oz) vegetable or meat stock
400g (14oz) pipe rigate
200g (7oz) parma ham, cut into strips
small handful fresh basil, in strips
freshly ground salt and pepper

1. Heat the oil in a large pan and sauté the onion until translucent.
2. Add the peas and the stock and cook for a few minutes or until the green peas are tender.
3. Cook the pipe rigate until al dente in a large pot of boiling salted water.
4. Strain the pasta and mix it into the green pea mixture together with the parma ham and the basil.
5. Grind a little salt and pepper over the top and serve right away in deep plates or bowls.

Linguine with salami

1 tbsp olive oil
1 red onion, minced
2 cloves garlic, minced
250g (9oz) salami (in a single link), skin removed and diced
1 red chilli pepper, seeded and minced
1 tbsp dried oregano
1 tbsp tomato puree
1 can of peeled and diced tomatoes (400g or 14oz)
400g (14oz) linguine
salt

1. Heat the oil in a large pan and sauté the onion and garlic for 1 minute. Add the diced salami and sauté another minute, stirring constantly.
2. Add the chilli pepper, oregano, tomato puree and tomato and simmer for 20 minutes or until everything has cooked down to a thick sauce.
3. When the sauce is almost done, cook the linguine until al dente in a large pot of boiling salted water.
4. Strain the linguine and toss with the tomato sauce. Portion onto plates or into bowls and serve immediately.

Oregano is an important culinary herb and plays a major role in Italian and Greek cuisine. The amount of sun the plant gets has a direct influence on its flavour. The name comes from the Greek word origanon, a combination of oros, meaning 'mountain' and the verb ganousthai, 'to delight in'

Fresh green peas should be eaten within 24 hours of harvest because the sugars are quickly converted to starch and the sweetness will disappear. Do not shell them until shortly before cooking.

Preserved anchovies

Preserved anchovies are an almost magical seasoning. You can toss in a filet if you think that a sauce – even a meat sauce – is missing something. The anchovy will almost completely 'melt' away, nothing left but that mysteriously full, potent flavour in your bolognese!

Fresh anchovies have a flavour similar to that of their big brother, the herring. Place them in salt for a few weeks or months and what you have is that distinct, unique anchovy flavour that drove the ancient Romans wild. Anchovies star in dishes like spaghetti alla puttanesca, but appear more often than you might think, often used 'under the radar', as a seasoning. The fish is cleaned as soon as it arrives in port, then placed between layers of coarse sea salt in storage vats. Weight is applied, pressing the little fillets slightly. The salt draws moisture out of the fish and ensures that the proteins in the meat solidify, a process similar to what happens when cooked. This vastly extends the fish's shelf life. The anchovies are left for about three months to age. It is during this time that the characteristic aroma, flavour and colour develop. They are then usually packed in oil, in those famous little tins, or turned into anchovy paste. In Italy, anchovies are also preserved whole in coarse sea salt, heads and all. They keep their flavour better this way, though are more difficult to prepare.

Fresh anchovies

Though most of the anchovy catch is immediately preserved, Italians also eat them fresh. These tasty little fish find their way into pasta, onto the grill, or are marinated as an antipasto.

Anyone who takes even a casual glance at a
map of Italy should not be surprised that
the country's cuisine puts such an emphasis on
fish and seafood. From the narrow, rocky coast
of Liguria and the Tuscan bays to the golden
beaches of Abruzzi and Apulia – not to men-
tion the island provinces of Sicily and Sardinia
– fresh seafood is everywhere. There is fresh
fish like seabass, sardines and red mullet,

Pasta with fish & seafood

there is octopus and squid, and all manner of shellfish. As well as the surrounding seas, there are also many lakes and rivers, where trout and other freshwater fish are caught. Inevitably, a good deal of this seafood finds its way into pasta dishes. In the south of Italy you will often find it combined with tomato sauces, like the Neapolitan pasta with tomatoes and tuna, venus clams or other shellfish. The com-bination of anchovies, broccoli and tomato is a classic from Apulia. In the north, seafood is often combined with cream sauces, like those chic Venetian dishes with scampi, spider crab and other shellfish, or modern classics with smoked salmon and cream. There are almost infinite variations upon these two elements, whether served as a traditional starter, light lunch or as a complete evening meal.

Linguine with scampi in garlic mustard sauce

400g (14oz) linguine
salt
1 tbsp olive oil
1 onion, chopped
2 cloves of garlic, minced
500g (18oz) raw scampi, peeled and deveined
1 tbsp garlic mustard
2 tomatoes, seeded and diced
100ml (3.5oz) crème fraîche
small handful of fresh basil, cut into strips

1. Cook the linguine until al dente in a large pot of boiling salted water.
2. While the pasta cooks, heat the oil in a pan and briefly sauté the onion and garlic.
3. Add the scampi and continue sautéing until they are just pink. Stir in the garlic mustard, tomatoes, crème fraîche and basil and heat everything through well.
4. Strain the pasta and mix it right into the scampi sauce.
5. Portion onto plates or into bowls and serve immediately.

You can find garlic mustard in specialty shops and well-stocked supermarkets. It tastes delicious. If you can't find garlic mustard for this recipe, simply substitute a good French mustard or other specialty type,such as tarragon or peppered.

Tortiglioni with spinach and olive tapenade

400g (14oz) tortiglioni
salt
500g (18oz) spinach, chopped
1 tbsp olive oil
1 shallot, minced

For the tapenade:
100g (3.5oz) green olives, pitted
1 can anchovy filets (50g or 1.75oz)
1 tbsp parsley, minced
1 tbsp capers
4 tbsp olive oil

1. Cook the tortiglioni until al dente in a large pot of boiling salted water.
2. While the pasta cooks, grind the ingredients for the tapenade in a blender or with an hand-held blender.
3. Heat the oil in a large pan or wok and sauté the shallot for approx. 20 seconds. Add the spinach. When the spinach has boiled down, remove from the heat.
4. Strain the tortiglioni and mix directly into the spinach mixture. Heat through well and divide over 4 plates. Serve the tapenade on the side.

There was a time when people were advised against reheating spinach after it had been cooked. The reasoning was that reheated spinach contained unusually large quantities of nitrite. This comes from a time when not everyone could afford their own refrigerator or freezer. With modern refrigeration technology, spinach can be quickly chilled, rendering this advice obsolete. However, it is still wise for small children, pregnant women and the elderly to be careful with spinach if not eaten fresh.

Tagliatelle with seabass and glasswort

400g (14oz) tagliatelle
salt
1l fish stock
4 × 100g (3.5oz) seabass filets
200g (7oz) glasswort (marsh samphire), blanched for 1 minute in boiling water

For the herb oil:
1 clove garlic
1 tbsp parsley, minced
1 tbsp basil, minced
1 tbsp chervil, minced
100ml (3.5oz) olive oil
100ml (3.5oz) maize-germ oil
salt and pepper

1. Cook the tagliatelle until al dente in a large pot of boiling salted water.
2. Meanwhile, bring the fish stock to the boil. Poach the seabass filets in the stock for approx. 10 minutes on low heat.
3. Remove the filets from the pot and cut each one in half. Set aside and keep warm.
4. Blend all the ingredients for the herb oil with an hand-held blender and add salt and pepper to taste.
5. Strain the pasta and return to the pot. Stir 2 tablespoons of the herb oil into the pasta and toss with the glasswort.
6. Portion onto plates and top with the pieces of seabass. Serve immediately, with the remaining herb oil on the side.

Glasswort season starts around the end of April or beginning of May and runs through August. Clean glasswort by removing the tough parts towards the bottom, if necessary, and briefly rinse under cold water. Never let glasswort sit in tap water. This plant is adapted to salt water and cannot tolerate fresh water.

Cravattine
with coquilles Saint-Jacques

400g (14oz) cravattine all'uovo

salt

2 tbsp olive oil

2 cloves of garlic, minced

half a red chilli pepper, seeded and minced

2 spring onions, minced

200ml (7oz) single cream

freshly grated pepper

16 scallops (coquilles Saint-Jacques or 'Jacob's shells')

1. Cook the cravattine until al dente in a large pot of boiling salted water.

2. Heat 1 tablespoon of the olive oil in a large frying pan and sauté the garlic and chilli pepper for about 30 seconds. Add the spring onion, stir well, then pour in the cream. Taste and add salt and pepper if needed.

3. Coat the scallops on both sides with the remaining olive oil. Heat a griddle or grill pan on high heat and cook the scallops for about 30 seconds to 1 minute on each side.

4. Strain the pasta and toss with the cream sauce.

5. Portion onto plates and top each serving with 4 scallops. Serve immediately.

Fresh scallops have a delectably sweet flavour and are at their best in simple dishes. Never keep scallops in water as they will absorb it like a sponge.

Fazzoletti with crab and cream sauce

1 tbsp olive oil
1 onion, chopped
3 cloves of garlic, minced
1 celery stalk, thinly sliced
1 dried chilli pepper, crumbled
250g (9oz) fresh crab meat
juice of 1 lemon
4 tbsp cooking cream
small handful of fresh oregano, coarsely chopped

For the pasta dough:
300g (10.5oz) Italian pasta flour (type '00'), sifted
3 eggs
half tsp salt

1. Put the flour in a pile and make a pit in the middle. Break the eggs into the pit and add the salt. Using a fork, stir carefully from the centre outwards until the flour is thoroughly mixed with the eggs. Knead for 10-15 minutes or until the dough has become soft and elastic. Cover in plastic wrap and set aside for 30 minutes to rest.

2. Heat the oil in a pan and sauté the onion, garlic, celery and chilli for 1 minute.

3. Roll the pasta dough out to a thin sheet and cut it into squares measuring 8cm x 8cm. Cook the fazzoletti squares until al dente in a large pot of boiling salted water. This should take about 4 minutes.

4. Remove the vegetable mixture from the heat and stir in the crab, lemon juice and cream.

5. Gently combine the fazzoletti with the sauce and sprinkle with the oregano.

According to nutritionists, pasta is actually better for you if cooked al dente than boiled until soft all the way through due to its lower GI value. GI stands for Glycemic Index and is a system for classifying carbohydrates according to how quickly they are burned off. The kind in al dente pasta are 'slow carbs', meaning the body absorbs them more slowly and evenly than other kinds. Slow carbs give you longer-lasting energy and are better for your figure.

Penne with fresh tuna and peppers

small handful of mint leaves, finely chopped juice of 1 lime
1 tbsp balsamic vinegar
2 tbsp olive oil
500g (18oz) fresh tuna, in small chunks
400g (14oz) penne rigate (Grand'Italia)
salt
1 sweet red pepper, cut into strips
1 sweet green pepper, cut into strips
1 sweet yellow pepper, cut into strips
100g (3.5oz) crimini or other brown button mushrooms, sliced
8 anchovy fillets (from the tin)
2 tbsp green olives, pitted
1 tbsp capers

1. Combine the mint, lime juice, balsamic vinegar and 1 tbsp olive oil. Marinate the pieces of tuna in the mixture for 30 minutes. Remove the tuna and pat dry.
2. Cook the penne until al dente in a large pot of boiling salted water.
3. While the pasta cooks, heat 1 tablespoon of olive oil in a large pan and sauté the pepper strips and mushroom slices for approx. 1 minute.
4. Add the anchovies and stir until dissolved. Add the olives, capers and tuna and sauté another minute. Stir in the marinade and heat well.
5. Strain the pasta and portion onto plates. Ladle the tuna mixture over the pasta and serve immediately.

Tuna spoils quickly due to its high fat and oil content. Fresh tuna steaks should be firm to the touch and have a somewhat meaty, not fishy, scent. Pat the steaks dry with a paper towel before cooking and be sure to eat as fresh as possible.

Conchiglie all'uovo with shrimp in creamy dill sauce

400g (14oz) conchiglie all'uovo
salt
fresh dill, for garnishing
For the dill and cream sauce:
200ml (7oz) single cream
250ml (7oz) fish stock
2 tbsp pernod
juice of 1 lime
small handful of fresh dill, chopped
300g (10.5oz) shrimp, peeled and cooked
freshly ground pepper

1. Cook the pasta until al dente in a large pot of boiling salted water.
2. While the pasta is cooking, pour the cream and fish stock into another pot and bring to a boil. Turn down to a simmer and cook the cream sauce on low heat for approx. 10 minutes or until reduced by half, stirring occasionally.
3. Stir the pernod, the lemon juice, dill and shrimp into the cream sauce, taste and add salt and pepper if needed.
4. Strain the pasta and mix into the sauce.
5. Portion onto plates, sprinkle with dill and serve immediately.

Pernod-Ricard is a French distilling company. Its most famous product is Ricard Pastis. This aperitif, made from star anise and herbal extracts, is also referred to colloquially as Ricard or Pernod.

Penne rigate with anchovies and broccoli

400g (14oz) penne rigate

salt

400g (14oz) broccoli, in small florets

1 onion, minced

2 cloves of garlic, minced

3 tbsp olive oil

4 tomatoes, seeded and cut into strips

50g (1.75oz) black olives, pitted

2 tbsp capers

1 tin anchovy filets (50g or 1.75oz)

1 spring onion, sliced

juice of 1 lemon

1 tbsp fresh oregano, coarsely chopped

1. Cook the penne until al dente in a large pot of boiling salted water.
2. While the pasta cooks, blanch the broccoli florets in a pot of boiling water for 2 minutes. Remove from the pot and strain.
3. Sauté the onion and garlic in the olive oil until translucent. Add the strips of tomato, the olives, capers, anchovies, spring onion and the broccoli and stir gently.
4. Strain the pasta and toss with the broccoli mixture.
5. Portion onto plates, drizzle with the lemon juice and sprinkle the chopped oregano over top. Serve immediately.

Lemon is not just a seasoning, it also works as a flavour enhancer, bringing out the taste of other ingredients. Like salt, a few drops of lemon juice can really bring a dish to life.

Lasagnette with salmon and crème fraîche-chive sauce

400g (14oz) lasagnette
salt
chives, for garnishing

For the crème fraîche and chive sauce:
250ml (1cup) crème fraîche
100ml (3.5oz) vegetable or fish stock
handful of chives, chopped
200g (7oz) smoked salmon, cut into strips
salt and pepper

1. Cook the lasagnette until al dente in a large pot of boiling salted water.
2. While the pasta cooks, heat the crème fraîche in a separate pot and stir in the stock, chives and smoked salmon. Heat well and add salt and pepper to taste.
3. Strain the pasta and toss with the sauce.
4. Portion the lasagnette into deep plates or bowls and serve immediately.

Fusilli with fresh salmon, watercress and horseradish

100ml (3.5oz) dry white wine
100ml (3.5oz) cooking cream
200ml (7oz) fish stock
1 small onion, minced
400g (14oz) fusilli
salt
2 tbsp horseradish (from the jar)
400g (14oz) fresh salmon fillets, in small chunks pepper
75g (2.5oz) watercress, coarsely chopped (set a few leaves aside for garnishing)

1. For the sauce: bring the wine, cream, fish stock and onion to a boil. Reduce the heat and simmer down to half the original quantity.
2. Cook the fusilli until al dente in a large pot of boiling salted water.
3. Stir the horseradish and salmon into the sauce and add salt and pepper to taste.
4. Strain the pasta and mix directly into the sauce.
5. Toss with the watercress. Portion onto plates or into bowls and garnish with the remaining watercress. Serve immediately.

The peppery flavour of watercress is a delightful addition to soups, salads, omelettes and quiches. Always go for light green, fresh-looking leaves and do not keep them longer than a day in the refrigerator. Watercress spoils remarkably fast.

La Taverna del mar
"LUCIO"

Spaghetti with bottarga

200ml (7oz) olive oil
6 cloves of garlic, peeled and cut in half
400g (14oz) spaghetti
approx. 40g (1.5oz) bottarga

1. Heat the oil in a pan and add the garlic halves. Cook on low heat until soft. Mash the garlic into the oil with the prongs of a fork.
2. Cook the spaghetti until al dente in a large pot of boiling salted water. Strain and toss with the garlic oil.
3. Portion the pasta onto plates and grate the bottarga over the top. Serve immediately.

Bottarga is a Sardinian speciality, consisting of the dried and salted roe of tuna or grey mullet. It is available in Italian food shops or other specialty stores. It is sometimes cut into thin slices as a deliciously salty antipasto.

Crisp-fried spaghetti with anchovies and bread crumbs

500g (18oz) spaghetti (or vermicelli)
2 tbsp olive oil
2 cloves of garlic, minced
10 anchovy filets
100g (3.5oz) bread crumbs, toasted in the oven
small handful parsley, coarsely chopped

1. Cook the spaghetti until al dente in a large pot of boiling salted water.
2. While the pasta cooks, heat the olive oil in a pan and sauté the garlic for 1 minute, without browning.
3. Stir in the anchovies and cook on low heat until dissolved to a paste.
4. Add the spaghetti and the bread crumbs to the pan and fry until crisp.
5. Portion into deep plates and sprinkle with the parsley. Serve immediately.

April 1st

"For those who love this dish, there's nothing like real home-grown spaghetti," commentator Richard Dimbleby tells television audiences in the fascinating BBC documentary "Spaghetti Picking in the Spring", broadcast in 1957. The programme is about the spaghetti harvest in Ticino, Switzerland, showing images of a farm family picking pounds of spaghetti from the trees. In Switzerland, spaghetti cultivation is "more of a family affair" in comparison to the "vast spaghetti plantations in the Po valley". The last weeks of March are a tense time for the spaghetti farmer, Dimbleby informs us, because a late frost can seriously impair the flavour. That the BBC received hundreds of telephone calls the next day (April 2nd) from viewers wanting to know how they could grow their own spaghetti went to show that pasta was still something of a novelty in 1950s England. "Simply place a sprig of spaghetti in a tin of tomato sauce and hope for the best," was the BBC's tongue-in-cheek reply.

Italian cheese

Cooking pasta without cheese is almost unthinkable. Freshly grated Parmesan, the 'king of cheeses' is not the only thing you'd be missing out on. Think about that rich, aromatic gorgonzola melting like velvet over hot gnocchi, or mascarpone giving mushroom and shellfish sauces their unmistakable creaminess, or fresh mozzarella, or crumbly sheep's cheese...

The cheese making tradition is almost as deeply rooted in Italy as pasta making. Each region has its own unique cheese varieties, most made from cow's and sheep's milk. The early Romans made their own cheese simply as a way of preserving the milk. There were all sorts of 'Italian' cheeses even before there was an Italy. These cheeses have been incorporated into various dishes since the first century BC. It was the medieval monasteries that perfected the art of cheese-making. Some varieties are still made today as they were in the Middle Ages. Italian cheeses are as varied as the Italian landscape. The verdant grasslands in the north are well suited to grazing cows whose milk is used to make the famous Parmesan cheese, among other types. The Alpine regions give us creamy taleggio and fontina, also from cow's milk. In central and southern Italy, sheep's cheese is dominant, the best-known being Pecorino. And in the swampy areas of the south live water buffalos – nobody knows how these animals ended up here – whose milk is used to make 'true' mozzarella, that is buffalo mozzarella.

Parmigiano-Reggiano
Parmesan, or properly Parmigiano-Reggiano, is so popular all over the world that around two million rounds of this cheese are produced annually. This number is even more startling when you consider that the cheese can only be produced in certain parts of Emilia-Romagna – and to strict standards. The quality is tested after a minimum ripening time of fourteen months. A special hammer is used, the sound of which, when struck against the rind, indicates what the cheese is like inside. A small piece is tasted. If the flavour is completely perfect, the genuine Parmigiano-Reggiano seal is burned into the rind, along with the year it was produced.   .

Grana
Grana is a general term for the hard cow's milk cheeses made in the Po valley. This includes Parmigiano Reggiano (Parmesan cheese) and Grana Padano. They are generally aged a long time (at least six months, though often a year or more), giving them a grainy texture and a fruity, intense flavour. Always grate it yourself; the stuff in the shaker has usually lost most of its flavour.

Gorgonzola
A rich-tasting, semi-soft blue cheese from Lombardy. *Gorgonzola dolce* is the younger variety, with a somewhat milder, sweeter flavour.

Mozzarella
Young, snow-white mozzarella balls are most authentic, and delicious, when made from buffalo milk. Buffalo mozzarella tastes fresher and considerably softer than cow's milk mozzarella, which has a tougher consistency.

Ricotta
Ricotta means 're-cooked', which is exactly how this cheese is produced. The whey (the liquid left over after production of other cheeses) is reheated, causing the residual solids to lump together, forming the curd-like consistency for which ricotta is known. These lumps are then strained and packaged without further processing.

Ricotta salata
Sicilian ricotta salata is produced much the same way as regular ricotta, the difference being that once the whey has been drained off, the remaining lumps are salted, then pressed. The taste is nothing like regular ricotta and the texture is much firmer and drier as well.

Mascarpone
In Italy, this fresh soft cheese is used much like cream is in other countries; it goes into both sweet and salty dishes.

Fontina
True fontina is produced in the Aosta valley. It is a smooth semi-soft cheese with a fresh, milky flavour when young and a slightly nutty overtone when aged several months. It melts well, making it an excellent choice for hot dishes and casseroles.

Pecorino
Pecorino is a general term for the sheep's cheeses traditionally produced in south and central Italy. They can be eaten when young, though they are usually sold well-aged and have a piquant and quite salty flavour. The most famous, of course, is Pecorino Romano, from Latium, though there are other varieties, such as Pecorino Sardo (from Sardinia), Pecorino Toscano, Pecorino Siciliano, et cetera.

A thick, creamy sauce lying atop fresh egg pasta like a velvet ribbon. This is most northern Italians' favourite pasta, setting them apart from southerners, who use more olive oil than butter and cream. Before refrigeration, dairy products were easier to keep in the north than in the heatof the south, and the northern grasslands were better suited to cattle grazing than the rocky south, where mostly sheep were kept. There are generally two types *of cream used in Italian cuisine: panna da cucina (cooking, or double, cream) and* panna da dolce or da montare (whipping cream). The first is mostly used, as the name implies, in pasta sauces and other warm dishes. It is thicker and contains more fat than normal whipping cream, making it ideal for delicious rich sauces like *all'Alfredo.* Most of the recipes in this book call for single

Pasta with cheese & cream

cream, however. Single cream is not nearly as fatty as panna or whipping cream (20% fat, compared to 30-35% or more in whipping cream and panna), takes the heat well and has a nice, well-rounded flavour. The result, of course, is somewhat thinner and lighter, but is better suited to modern tastes (and diets). Not to say you can't toss in a little panna now and again if you really want to go all out. You can also experi-

ment with various cheeses (besides the indispensable grated Parmesan or pecorino) to get just the right creaminess in your sauce. And if you're concerned about calories, just substitute ricotta; it has only five to twenty percent fat, a big difference when you consider that mascarpone often has ninety percent.

All of the following recipes make four servings.

Stringhetti with saffron

(V)

100ml (3.5oz) dry white wine
small pinch of saffron
400g (14oz) stringhetti all'uovo (Grand'Italia)
250ml (1cup) single cream
100g (3.5oz) Parmesan cheese
1 egg yolk

1. Heat the white wine in a pan. Stir in the saffron, keep on low heat a few minutes and allow to infuse.
2. Meanwhile, cook the stringhetti until al dente in a large pot of boiling salted water.
3. Add the cream and Parmesan cheese to the wine and saffron. When the cheese has melted, remove the pan from the heat and whisk the egg yolk into the sauce, making sure it reaches an even consistency.
4. Strain the stringhetti and mix directly into the sauce. Portion into bowls and serve immediately.

ⓥ Three-cheese lasagne

1 tbsp olive oil plus extra for greasing

1 onion, finely chopped

3 cloves of garlic, pressed

150g (5oz) mushrooms, thinly sliced

1 red chilli pepper, seeded and minced

1 sweet red pepper, diced

1 sweet green pepper, diced

2 tins peeled Italian tomatoes (400g (14oz) each)

100ml (3.5oz) tomato juice (from the tomato tins)

salt and pepper

1 package lasagne leaves (500g or 18oz), pre-cooked if necessary (most brands do not require pre-cooking)

100g (3.5oz) soft goat's cheese, crumbled

100g (3.5oz) hard cheese, grated

100g (3.5oz) Parmesan cheese, grated

1. Preheat the oven to 200°C (400°F or gas mark 6).
2. Heat the oil in a pan and sauté the onion until translucent. Add the garlic and cook a minute or two longer.
3. Stir in the mushroom, chilli, and red and green peppers. Fry for another minute on high heat, stirring constantly. Then add the tomatoes and tomato juice. Stir well, reduce the heat and simmer gently for approx. 5 minutes. Add salt and pepper to taste.
4. Grease a casserole dish with olive oil and coat the bottom with a thin layer of the tomato sauce. Place a layer of lasagne sheets over this, followed by another layer of sauce. Cover this with a thin layer of goat's cheese, followed by another layer of lasagne, another layer of tomato sauce, and a layer of hard cheese. Continue filling the dish in this order, ending with a layer of tomato sauce. Top with Parmesan cheese.
5. Bake for approx. 30 minutes or until golden brown and well-cooked.

Always buy the best quality tinned tomatoes available. One way of checking quality is to look for the country of origin on the tin. Italians are quite picky when it comes to their tomatoes, so if the tin says 'Made in Italy', that's a good indication of quality.

ⓥ Lasagne with mozzarella and béchamel

1 package lasagne leaves (500g or 18oz), pre-cooked if necessary (most brands do not require pre-cooking)

salt

1 tbsp olive oil plus extra for greasing

1 onion, minced

2 cloves of garlic, minced

1 aubergine, cubed

1 sweet green pepper, diced

1 spring onion, sliced into ringlets

small handful of basil leaves, coarsely chopped

3 mozzarella balls, sliced

For the béchamel sauce:

40g (1.5oz) butter

40g (1.5oz) wheat flour, sifted

200ml (7oz) whole milk, warm

200ml (7oz) vegetable stock

salt and pepper

pinch of nutmeg

1. Preheat the oven to 200°C (400°F or gas mark 6).
2. For the béchamel sauce, melt the butter in a pan and add the flour. Stirring constantly, add the warm milk and vegetable stock a little at a time until you have a nice smooth sauce. Add salt and pepper and a pinch of nutmeg to taste. Remove the pan from the heat and set aside for later.
3. Heat the oil in a pan and sauté the onion and garlic for approx. 1 minute. Add the aubergine cubes and cook on high another minute. Add the pepper, the spring onion and the basil and cook another minute, stirring constantly.
4. Grease a casserole dish with olive oil and place a layer of lasagne sheets on the bottom. Cover the lasagne sheets with a layer of vegetables, followed by the mozzarella slices, then a thin layer of the béchamel sauce. Continue filling the casserole dish by layering the pasta, vegetables, mozzarella and béchamel in this order, ending with the mozzarella and béchamel on top. Bake for approx 30 minutes or until golden brown and well-cooked.

Pappardelle with asparagus carbonara

10 green asparagus, cleaned and sliced
into diagonal pieces
1 tbsp olive oil
100g (3.5oz) cooked ham, in strips
125ml (0.5 cup) single cream
100g (3.5oz) Parmesan cheese, grated
2 egg yolks
400g (14oz) pappardelle all'uovo (Grand'Italia)
freshly grated black pepper

1. Boil the asparagus for 5 minutes, remove and rinse under cold water to cool
2. Heat the oil in a pan and sauté the strips of ham together with the cooked asparagus for 1 minute.
3. In a mixing bowl, combine the cream, the cheese and the egg yolks.
4. Meanwhile, cook the pasta until al dente in a large pot of boiling salted water. Strain the pasta well (save some of the water), and return it to the pot.
5. Toss the ham and asparagus with the hot pasta. Add the egg and cream mixture and stir well to evenly distribute the sauce over the pasta and other ingredients. If the sauce is too thick, add some of the pasta water which has been set aside.
6. Portion the pappardelle onto plates and grind black pepper over the top. Serve immediately.

If you see the phrase 'all'uovo' after the name of a pasta, this means that egg was used for the dough. Pasta all'uovo is heartier and richer in flavour than normal pasta and is best combined with soft, delicate sauces.

Garlic

Garlic takes the spotlight in dishes like *spaghetti aglio e olio*, where it is the principle seasoning. It is also a component of many other pasta sauces, though takes a more subdued role, rounding out the general flavour. The delectable Italian variety, with its violet flecks and succulent cloves, is a daily staple, particularly in the south.

Keep your eyes open for other garlic varieties besides the 'standard' white bulbs stocked in most grocery stores. There are literally hundreds of varieties, ranging from white and light green to pink and purple, all of various shapes and sizes. There are also hybrid 'solo garlic' bulbs, which are composed of just one big clove – no extra peeling necessary. If you don't go through the garlic as quickly as most Italians do, it's perhaps best to buy it by the bulb rather than in a net, because garlic is best used fresh. If you do decide to keep garlic for extended periods, store it in a cool, dry place – not in the refrigerator.

Bitter?

Some people claim they do not like garlic because it has a bitter taste. Good, fresh garlic should not taste bitter in the least. Only when a bulb of garlic is past its prime and the cloves get soft or turn green with shoots does the fresh, piquant taste changes into an unpleasantly bitter off-flavour. Keep a good eye on garlic when sautéing because it burns very fast. This can also lead to bitterness.

Garlic breath

Afraid of getting that infamous garlic breath? Fresh parsley is the best thing for neutralising the scent of garlic. Simply pluck off a generous mouthful and chew. Chewing on a coffee bean is also effective.

Mincing and pressing

Garlic is easy to peel if you first crush the whole clove. Place the flat edge of a wide knife on top of the clove and press down firmly with your palm. The peel should pop right off and the garlic is ready to chop (or press). Remember: the juice from pressed garlic gives a stronger flavour than when simply chopped or sliced. Many people prefer the latter two methods for this reason. Many Italian recipes call for a whole clove, which is sautéed with other ingredients, then removed. This provides a milder flavour, as does slow-stewing, as in a ragù.

ⓥ Tortiglioni with tomato and parmesan

400g (14oz) tortiglioni
salt
1 tbsp olive oil
4 tomatoes, quartered
1 red onion, cut into half rings
100g (3.5oz) Parmesan cheese, grated

1. Cook the tortiglioni until al dente in a large pot of boiling salted water.
2. While the pasta cooks, heat the olive oil in a pan and sauté the tomatoes and onion for approx. 5 minutes on medium to high heat. Remove from the heat and, using a hand-held blender, puree to a semi-smooth but still slightly chunky sauce.
3. Strain the tortiglioni and mix into the sauce. Portion into bowls and top with a layer of grated Parmesan cheese. Serve immediately.

ⓥ Tagliatelle all'uovo with gorgonzola and sage

400g (14oz) tagliatelle all'uovo
salt
100ml (3.5oz) single cream
200g (7oz) gorgonzola, crumbled
small handful of sage leaves, chopped
(set some leaves aside for garnishing)

1. Cook the tagliatelle until al dente in a large pot of boiling salted water.
2. While the pasta cooks, heat the cream in a small saucepan. Add the gorgonzola. When the gorgonzola has melted, stir in the sage and remove from the heat.
3. Strain the tagliatelle and immediately toss with the gorgonzola sauce. Divide over 4 plates, garnish with the sage leaves and serve immediately.

Onions and shallots are the onion plant's underground nutrient reserves. Their sharp scent and tear-jerking capabilities are a means of defence. Red onions are milder and sweeter in flavour than white or yellow onions

Sage, with its powdery green hue and soft, oblong leaves, is arguably the most attractive of all herbs. This is one reason why it appears so often as a garden ornamental. Sage is also frost resistant and can stand up to a little neglect on the part of the gardener. This makes it the ideal herb for home cultivation.

Ricotta gnocchi

1 tbsp olive oil
1 pint cheery tomatoes, halved
1 clove of garlic, minced
half a red chilli pepper, seeded and cut into thin strips
100g (3.5oz) Parmesan cheese, grated
small handful of basil leaves, cut into strips

For the gnocchi:
400g (14oz) ricotta
100g (3.5oz) Italian flour *(semola di grano duro)*
plus extra for dusting
2 egg yolks
salt and pepper

1. In a large mixing bowl, combine all the ingredients for the gnocchi and knead on a floured surface until you have a dough of even consistency.
2. Roll the dough up into cylinders with a diameter of approx. 2 cm. Cut the rolls into 2cm. diagonal pieces.
3. Cook the gnocchi a little at a time in a large pot of boiling salted water. As soon as they float to the top, remove the gnocchi with a skimmer or sieve. Place them in a colander to drain.
4. Heat the oil in a pan and briefly sauté the gnocchi on all sides. Add the cherry tomatoes, garlic and chilli pepper and keep on the heat until the tomatoes soften.
5. Divide the gnocchi over 4 plates or bowls and serve with basil and Parmesan cheese.

Italian pomodori

A sun-ripened, fire-red tomato, just plucked from the vine by the time-worn hand of an Italian farmer. You sink your teeth in and the tender fruit is sweeter, juicier and simply that much more flavourful than any other tomato you have ever tasted.

It's little wonder that the tomato, first brought to Europe as a novelty item by early Spanish explorers, has taken on such an important role in Italian cuisine. The soil, the climate, everything is perfect for the cultivation of what may well be the most attractive and flavourful tomatoes in the world. When you think of pasta, you almost automatically associate it with tomato sauce, from the simplest marinara with little more than garlic and herbs for seasoning, to those rich tomato-cream sauces and hearty winter meat and game ragù. Whatever sauce you decide to make, only use fresh tomatoes if they are good and ripe. Only then will they come close to the pure Italian tomato taste which is so important for the dish's overall cohesion. If you do not have access to full, fresh red tomatoes, do not hesitate to reach for some good Italian tinned tomatoes. Tomatoes keep their flavour fairly well even in the tin, and aromatic pomodori pelati far exceed their watery, unripe cousins.

Pomodori secchi

A selection of processed tomato products are also used in Italian cuisine besides fresh tomatoes, with excellent results. 'Sun-dried' tomatoes, contrary to what the name implies, are most often factory dried. This doesn't mean they are any less flavourful, however. Pomodori secchi (the phrase simply means 'dried tomatoes') should first be soaked in a little hot water if using the dry, bag variety. The oil-cured kind can be used straight from the jar.

Home-dried tomatoes

When summertime comes and the greengrocers are overflowing with inexpensive fresh tomatoes, then carpe diem: don't miss the chance to make your own pomodori secchi. At this time of year, tomatoes are often too ripe to be kept any longer and need to be preserved. Buy a few bagfuls and cut each one down the middle. Sprinkle with salt, pepper, and olive oil, then place them cut-side up in a warm oven at 50 - 100°C (120 - 210°F or below gas mark 1). Leave the door slightly ajar to allow the steam escape. Depending on your oven and the type of tomatoes, the drying process will take five to seven hours, but your patience will be well rewarded with the most delicious home-dried tomatoes: tender, sweet, delicious!

Tomato puree, passata and sugocasa

Tomato puree is extremely concentrated; you only need a little to add a lot of colour and flavour to a dish. *Passata* consists of raw tomatoes that have been pureed and sifted to remove the skins and seeds. It is usually sold in small cartons. *Sugocasa is a pure unseasoned tomato sauce made from* coarsely chopped tomatoes. It is a suitable alternative for fresh tomatoes because it consists entirely of freshly harvested tomatoes and no artificial additives.

Maccheroncini with pancetta and mascarpone

400g (14oz) maccheroncini

salt

1 tbsp olive oil

1 clove of garlic, minced

200g (7oz) pancetta, cut into strips

200ml (7oz) single cream

200ml (7oz) chicken stock

200g (7oz) mascarpone

1. Cook the maccheroncini until al dente in a large pot of boiling salted water.
2. While the pasta cooks, heat the olive oil in a pan and sauté the garlic until golden brown. Add the pancetta and fry, stirring constantly, until crisp.
3. Add the single cream and chicken stock to the pancetta, stir well and bring to a boil. Reduce the heat and simmer gently for 2 minutes. Add the mascarpone and stir until dissolved.
4. Strain the maccheroncini and mix with the sauce. Portion onto plates and serve immediately.

ⓥ Pipe rigate with pecorino walnut sauce

400g (14oz) pipe rigate (Grand'Italia)

salt

1 tbsp olive oil

2 cloves of garlic, minced

200g (7oz) walnuts, finely chopped

100ml (3.5oz) single cream

small handful of basil leaves, chopped

100g (3.5oz) pecorino, grated

1. Cook the pipe rigate until al dente in a large pot of boiling salted water.
2. While the pasta cooks, heat the olive oil in a pan and sauté the garlic until golden brown. Add the chopped walnuts and cook another 2 minutes.
3. Pour the single cream over the walnuts, stir well and simmer gently for a few minutes. Stir the basil and pecorino into the walnut sauce and heat well, stirring constantly.
4. Strain the pipe rigate and mix with the pecorino walnut sauce.
5. Portion into deep plates or bowls and serve immediately.

There isn't just one single type of cream but a plethora of varieties with widely diverse fat contents. The best-known kinds are: coffee cream (20% fat), sour cream (10-20%), demi crème fraîche (15%), crème fraîche (20-35%), clotted cream (55% +), double cream (48% +), pasteurised whipping cream (30-35%), sterilised whipping cream (35%), reduced fat whipping cream (25%) and single cream (20%). Most of the recipes in this book call for single cream. Feel free to substitute whipping cream or crème fraîche for a richer (and heavier) flavour.

Walnuts are rich in alpha-linolenic acid, the vegetable version of the essential omega-3 fatty acid. Omega-3, also found in fish, reduces the cholesterol level in your bloodstream and is also essential for good vision and proper brain metabolism. Walnuts also contain arginine, an amino acid which the body converts to nitric oxide, which in turn helps keep artery walls flexible and elastic and fat content in the blood under control.

ⓥ Whole-grain spaghetti with goat's cheese and roasted peppers

2 sweet red peppers
2 sweet yellow peppers
2 sweet green peppers
1 tbsp olive oil
3 cloves of garlic, minced
1 tbsp balsamic vinegar
400g (14oz) whole-grain spaghetti (spaghetti integrali Grand'Italia)
150g (5oz) soft goat's cheese
small handful of parsley, coarsely chopped

1. Preheat the oven to 200°C (400°F or gas mark 6).
2. Place the peppers in a casserole dish and bake for approx. 30 minutes.
3. Cover the dish with foil or a tea towel and return to the oven, heat off. When cool enough to handle, remove the stems, seeds and the skins (these should slide right off). Save the juice and slice the peppers into thin strips.
4. Heat the olive oil in a pan and sauté the garlic for 1 minute, without browning. Carefully stir in the pepper strips, the reserved juice and the balsamic vinegar.
5. Cook the spaghetti until al dente in a large pot of boiling salted water. Strain and mix with the sauce.
6. Portion the pasta into 4 deep plates. Crumble the goat's cheese over the top and sprinkle with parsley. Serve immediately.

ⓥ Penne with pear, pistachio and gorgonzola

4 dessert pears
1 tbsp fresh lemon juice
400g (14oz) penne
salt
1.5 tbsp butter
1 tsp sugar
2 tbsp vodka
200g (7oz) gorgonzola, in small cubes
small handful of parsley, finely chopped
2 tbsp pistachios, coarsely chopped

1. Peel and core the pears. Cut them into small cubes and sprinkle with the lemon juice.
2. Cook the penne until al dente in a large pot of boiling salted water.
3. While the pasta cooks, melt the butter in a large pan and add the pear cubes and sugar. Stir in the vodka and a pinch of salt. Briefly cook on high heat to reduce the alcohol.
4. Strain the penne, reserving 2 tablespoons of the water.
5. Stir the penne, including the 2 tablespoons of pasta water, into the pear mixture. Add the gorgonzola, half of the parsley and half of the pistachios.
6. Portion the pasta into deep plates or bowls and sprinkle with the remaining pistachios and parsley. Serve immediately.

ⓥ Pipe rigate with ricotta nut sauce

400g (14oz) pipe rigate
salt
1 tbsp olive oil
200g (7oz) cashew nuts, finely ground
100g (3.5oz) pine nuts, finely ground plus
1 tbsp whole
1 clove of garlic, pressed
200g (7oz) ricotta
100ml (3.5oz) single cream
100g (3.5oz) Parmesan cheese
handful of rocket, chopped
freshly ground black pepper

1. Cook the pipe rigate until al dente in a large pot of boiling salted water.
2. While the pasta cooks, heat the oil in a large pan. Add the ground cashews and pine nuts and sauté approx. 2 minutes, stirring constantly. Add the garlic and cook another minute.
3. Stir in the ricotta, the cream, the Parmesan cheese, the remaining pine nuts and the chopped rocket. Grind a little black pepper over the top.
4. Strain the pipe rigate and stir right into the nut and cheese sauce. Heat well and portion into bowls. Serve immediately.

The appearance of pears can sometimes be deceptive. Many of the over 5,000 varieties are grainy and of inferior flavour, with good-looking fruits often disappointing in flavour and texture while ugly-looking ones taste delicious. Try Doyenne du Comice, Conference or a similar dessert variety for this recipe.

Fettuccine with spinach and fontina

400g (14oz) fettuccine
salt
1 tbsp olive oil
1 shallot, finely chopped
400g (14oz) spinach, finely chopped
8 dried tomatoes, cut into strips and soaked
2 tbsp pine nuts, toasted in a dry pan on very low heat
200g (7oz) fontina, cut into small cubes

1. Cook the fettuccine until al dente in a large pot of boiling salted water.
2. While the pasta cooks, heat the olive oil in a pan and sauté the shallot until translucent. Add the spinach and cook on high heat until it just begins to boil down. Add the soaked tomato strips and the pine nuts and cook another minute, stirring constantly. Remove the pan from the heat.
3. Strain the fettuccine and toss with the spinach mixture and the fontina cubes.
4. Portion the pasta onto plates and serve immediately.

Many chefs swear by the shallot's delicate flavour. Compared to normal onions, shallots are much easier to digest. The only drawback is that peeling and cutting them is harder on the eyes.

Balsamic vinegar

Aceto balsamico tradizionale di Modena

This 'balsam-like' vinegar is produced in Modena with the help of special wooden barrels and a whole lot of time and was once ascribed medicinal value. Silky smooth, with a complex aroma that can't be duplicated. Add just a few drops to highlight the simplest of pastas.

True aceto balsamico is something you won't often find outside of gourmet food stores. Granted, every supermarket stocks some vinegar labelled as balsamic. Do not be fooled: these impostors have little or nothing to do with the real stuff. Authentic aceto balsamico tradizionale di Modena is produced from the concentrated must of white trebbiano grapes, aged for decades (often half a century) in a series of chestnut-, cherry-, ash-, mulberry-, and juniper-wood barrels, each one smaller than the last. These vats are stored in draughty attics, deliberately exposed to extremes of heat and cold. The vats are kept only two-thirds full, allowing oxygen to interact with the vinegar. Over time, a large proportion of the liquid evaporates, leaving an intensely concentrated vinegar. The result is dark brown and velvety smooth, with the consistency of syrup and a flavour of unequalled complexity. Tasty enough to sip from a demitasse!

Tradizionale

The problem is that the aceto balsamico designation is not very well protected. If it were, supermarkets would not be allowed to offer up any old brown vinegar as true balsamic. Not to say that there's necessarily anything wrong with these vinegars; they are usually perfectly decent wine vinegars which have been mixed with caramel for a darker colour and sweeter flavour. What they lack is the decades-long barrel ageing, the deliciously complex flavour and viscous consistency which are the hallmarks of true balsamic. The designation di Modena on the label, contrary to popular belief, is no certificate of origin. Tradizionale, on the other hand, is: any vinegar with this word in its title must be wood-aged for at least twelve years.

Quality

In some specialty shops, you can find aceto which is not 'tradizionale' but still wood-aged and of good quality. Good aceto has a syrupy consistency and is free of all colourings and other additives. Sometimes you just have to test a few. The price can be an indicator also – a small (usually 100 ml, or 3.5 oz) bottle of good aceto balsamico will cost you fifteen or twenty pounds (thirty or forty US dollars); with true, authentic tradizionale easily running upwards of fifty pounds... Think of it like buying jewellery – only tastier. A few well-placed drops will make all the difference in fresh dishes and simple sauces, but be careful not to overwhelm the precious flavour with too many other ingredients; you would be committing a culinary sin. For most pasta sauces, a less expensive variety should more than suffice.

Cold pasta salads with vegetables, chicken or seafood – these most certainly are not traditionally Italian. Pasta salad probably rose out of Australian fusion cuisine towards the end of the last century. These days pasta salads are also served in Italy, usually dressed with olive oil and vinegar. Short pasta is more popular than the long varieties for these dishes because it combines well with coarsely cut vegetables (usually the same size as the pasta itself). After boiling, briefly rinse the pasta off under cold water from the tap. This is important for letting the pasta cool quickly, otherwise it will continue to soften in its own heat. Rinsing also removes surface starch, which will become pasty in a cold salad (in warm pasta dishes this same starch helps to keep the sauce on: so only rinse pasta if you intend on using it

Pasta salads

cold, not warm!). Do not let the pasta sit in the water; strain it well and immediately toss it with olive oil or dressing (if using mayonnaise-based dressings, wait until the pasta is good and cool to add them). Pasta salads are wonderfully eclectic and nourishing. You can also keep them for some time without refrigeration, even after they've been tossed with the dressing – unless of course they contain fresh meat or seafood.

This makes them ideal for taking along to a picnic, or as a side dish at a barbecue.

All of the following recipes make four servings.

ⓥ Penne with aged cheese and avocado

400g (14oz) penne
salt
200g (7oz) hard cheese, in small cubes
1 red onion, cut into half rings
4 tomatoes, seeded and cut into small chunks
small handful of fresh coriander leaves, chopped
1 ripe avocado, in small cubes
juice of 2 limes

1. Cook the penne until al dente in a large pot of boiling salted water.
2. Briefly rinse the penne under cold running water and strain well in a colander. Place in a large mixing bowl when dry.
3. Mix in the cheese cubes, the red onion, tomato slices, coriander and avocado. Add lime juice to taste.

Mezzi rigatoni with snow peas and tuna

400g (14 oz) mezzi rigatoni
salt
1 tbsp olive oil
1 onion, minced
2 cloves of garlic, pressed
4 tomatoes, seeded and cut into small chunks
200 g (7 oz) snow peas, boiled until just tender (let them cool)
12 black olives, pitted and halved
1 tin of tuna in oil, drained
small handful of basil leaves, chopped

1. Cook the mezzi rigatoni until al dente in a large pot of boiling salted water.
2. While the pasta cooks, heat the olive oil in a pan and sauté the garlic for 1 minute. Remove from the heat.
3. Briefly rinse the mezzi rigatoni under cold running water and strain well in a colander. Place into a large mixing bowl.
4. Toss the pasta with the sautéed onion and garlic, the tomato, snow peas, olives, tuna and basil.
5. Serve in small bowls.

There are more than 500 varieties of avocado, some no larger than your thumb, others (particularly those grown in the Caribbean) weighing close to two pounds. The best method of cutting an avocado is to make an incision down the whole length, cutting through the fruit but around the pit. Take a half in each hand and pull them apart while slightly twisting each half in opposite directions.

The easiest way to pit an olive is to place it on a flat surface and press down with a metal spatula or other flat implement, rubbing back and forth a little. The pit should then be easy to remove.

Fusilli bucati with bresaola and rocket

400g (14oz) fusilli bucati (Grand'Italia)
100g (3.5oz) bresaola, in thin strips
150g (5oz) rocket
3 tbsp pine nuts, toasted in a dry pan on
very low heat
2 cloves of garlic, minced
100g (3.5oz) Parmesan cheese, grated
4 tbsp olive oil

1. Cook the pasta until al dente in a large pot of boiling salted water. Rinse under cold running water.
2. For the pesto: grind the rocket, pine nuts, garlic and cheese, in a food processor, pouring the olive oil in last of all.
3. Toss the cooled pasta with the pesto and bresaola and serve as a salad.

The question of whether a plant needs gravity to grow properly was finally answered by the astronaut André Kuipers during his 2004 space flight. He grew rocket from seed and observed that the sprouts seemed to grow out in all directions without any clear structure. The lesson learned: a plant does need gravity to determine its direction of growth.

Black linguine with pulpo salad

1 small pulpo (fresh octopus)
salt
5 tbsp olive oil
50ml (1.75oz) dry white wine
1 red onion, cut into rings
half a sweet red pepper, diced
half a sweet yellow pepper, diced
1 clove of garlic, pressed
juice of 1 lemon
sprig of rosemary, leaves finely chopped
sprig of thyme, leaves finely chopped
10 black olives, pitted and chopped
400g (14oz) black linguine

1. Bring a large pot of water to a boil. Add salt and drop in the pulpo, whole. Reduce the heat and cook for approx. 1 hour. The pulpo is done when you can easily stick a knife into the thickest part.

2. Briefly rinse the cooked pulpo under cold running water and remove the slimy substance from between the tentacles. Slice the pulpo into small pieces.

3. In a large bowl, whisk together olive oil and white wine for the dressing. Mix in the pieces of pulpo, the pepper, garlic, lemon juice, rosemary, thyme and olives. Add a little salt and, if necessary, lemon juice to taste (the dish should be slightly tart in flavour). Let sit for at least 2 hours, though overnight is best. This will allow the flavours to combine.

4. Cook the linguine until al dente in a large pot of boiling salted water.

5. Briefly rinse the pasta under cold running water and strain well in a colander.

6. Portion the cooled linguine onto plates and top with the pulpo salad.

Pulpo is the Spanish word for octopus. The meat of a large octopus with thick tentacles can be quite tough. The Spaniards' early answer to this was to throw the animal against a cliff a few times. Fortunately for us, freezing has the same result.

Gnocchi salad with fresh crab and rocket

400g (14oz) gnocchi (the noodles, not the dumplings)
200g (7oz) fresh crab meat
2 cloves of garlic, minced
small handful of fresh chives, chopped
50g (1.75oz) rocket, chopped
juice of 2 limes
1 tbsp olive oil
salt and pepper

1. Cook the gnocchi until al dente in a large pot of boiling salted water.
2. While the pasta cooks, mix the crab meat with the garlic, chives, rocket and lime juice. Add the oil and stir well. Add salt and pepper to taste.
3. Briefly rinse the gnocchi under cold running water and strain well in a colander.
4. Mix the pasta into the crab mixture and let stand for approx. 30 minutes for the flavours to combine. Divide over 4 plates and serve.

Rocket contains a large amount of vitamin C but also has a high nitrate content. For this reason, it should not be eaten in excessive quantities. The recommended maximum daily allowance of nitrate is 260mg per day for a person weighing 70kg. This works out to only about 20 grams of rocket.

Sweet (bell) peppers belong to the same family as chilli peppers. Sweet red peppers are simply green peppers which have been allowed to ripen. Yellow, orange and purple peppers are separate varieties.

Mezzi rigatoni with chicken and white asparagus

400g (14oz) mezzi rigatoni
salt
1 tbsp olive oil
2 cloves of garlic, minced
200g (7oz) chicken filets, diced
1 sweet yellow pepper, diced
1 pint cherry tomatoes, halved
500g (18oz) white asparagus, peeled, cut into segments and cooked until just tender.
small handful of fresh chives, chopped

For the balsamic dressing:
1 egg yolk
1 tsp. mustard
1 tsp. honey
100ml (3.5oz) vegetable stock
1 tbsp balsamic vinegar
5 tbsp maize-germ oil
salt

1. Cook the mezzi rigatoni until al dente in a large pot of boiling salted water.
2. While the pasta cooks, heat the olive oil in a pan and briefly sauté the garlic. Add the chicken and cook for approx. 2 minutes or until golden brown and cooked well.
3. For the balsamic dressing, blend the egg yolks, mustard, honey, stock and vinegar with a hand-held blender. Add the oil in a slow, thin stream as you blend. This should help the oil emulsify, giving a nice, smooth consistency. Taste, adding salt if needed. Add extra honey or oil if you think the dressing needs it.
4. Briefly rinse the mezzi rigatoni under cold running water and strain in a colander. Place in a large mixing bowl when dry.
5. Add the cooked chicken, the sweet pepper, tomatoes, asparagus and chives to the pasta. Pour the dressing on and carefully toss everything together.

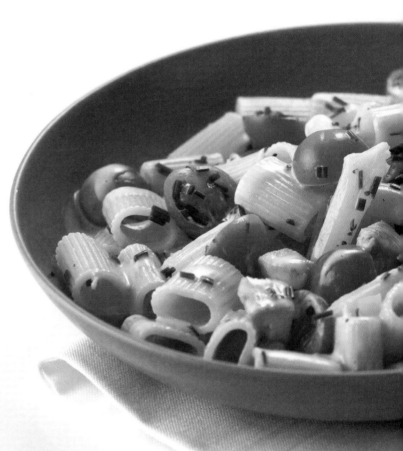

Fusilli with salmon and seafood

400g (14oz) fusilli
salt
1 tbsp olive oil
100g (3.5oz) baby octopus
100g (3.5oz) salmon filet, diced
12 raw scampi, peeled and deveined
100g (3.5oz) fresh crab meat
1 red onion, sliced into half rings
1 spring onion, sliced into thin ringlets
12 black olives, pitted
2 tbsp full-fat yoghurt
1 tbsp balsamic vinegar
small handful of dill, coarsely chopped +
extra for garnishing

1. Cook the gnocchi until al dente in a large pot of boiling salted water.
2. While the pasta cooks, heat the olive oil in a pan and sauté the baby octopus for approx. 2 minutes. Add the salmon and scampi and cook another minute. Remove from the heat.
3. Carefully stir the crab, red onion, spring onion and olives into the seafood mixture and set aside to cool.
4. Briefly rinse the fusilli under cold running water and strain in a colander. Place in a large mixing bowl when dry.
5. Whisk together a dressing of yoghurt, vinegar and dill, adding salt to taste.
6. Toss the pasta with the seafood mixture and pour the dressing over top. Serve on deep plates and garnish with extra dill.

Dill plays an important role in the cuisines of Russia, Germany, Poland, Scandinavia and the Baltic states. One of the best-known recipes incorporating dill is the Swedish gravad lax, a marinated salmon dish. Dill is never cooked with the other ingredients as exposure to extreme heat will make it lose its pronounced anise-like flavour. All parts of the dill plant are aromatic, though the seeds taste somewhat bitter.

Penne salad with tuna tapenade

400g (14oz) penne
salt

For the tuna tapenade:
100g (3.5oz) black olives, pitted and finely chopped
1 tbsp capers, finely chopped
10 anchovy fillets (from the tin), finely chopped
1 tin of tuna in oil, drained
100ml (3.5oz) olive oil
4 sun-dried tomatoes in oil, finely chopped
2 tbsp chopped fresh basil
1 tbsp lemon juice

1. Cook the penne until al dente in a large pot of boiling salted water.
2. Briefly rinse the penne under cold running water and strain in a colander. Place in a large mixing bowl when dry.
3. Combine all the ingredients for the tapenade and spoon over the pasta. Serve the pasta salad in small bowls.

ⓥ Orecchiette with beans and raisins

1 tbsp white wine vinegar
1 tbsp sugar
100ml (3.5oz) vegetable stock
1 tbsp olive oil
2 tbsp raisins
400g (14oz) lima beans (tinned)
200g (7oz) haricots verts, boiled until just tender (rinse cool)
1 red onion, cut into half rings
half a red chilli pepper, seeded and sliced into thin ringlets
small handful of parsley, minced
400g (14oz) orecchiette
salt and freshly ground pepper

1. For the dressing, combine the white wine vinegar, sugar and stock in a small saucepan. Place on low heat, stirring until the sugar has dissolved. Remove from the heat and pour into a large mixing bowl.
2. Stir in the oil, raisins, lima beans, haricots, red onion, chilli pepper and parsley and let marinade for approx. 30 minutes.
3. Meanwhile, cook the orecchiette until al dente in a large pot of boiling salted water.
4. Briefly rinse the pasta under cold running water and strain in a colander.
5. Mix the pasta into the bean mixture and add salt and freshly ground pepper to taste. Serve in small bowls.

Raisins consist of 90% sugar by weight. Half of this is fructose, the other glucose. These sugars may crystallise if kept for extended periods, giving the raisins a grainy taste. Place the raisins in some manner of liquid (alcohol, fruit juice, tea or boiling water) to soak. This will redissolve the crystallized sugars.

Olives & capers

Throw a handful of olives and a few tablespoons of capers into any simple tomato sauce and you're not far off from having a real delicacy. Add aubergine and a little sweet bell pepper and you have the sauce for *spaghetti alla siracusana*, or anchovies *for alla puttanesca*. Olives and capers automatically give any dish a Mediterranean feel.

Try eating an olive right off the tree and you will be in for a bitter surprise. Olives are only edible after being cured, usually in salt water. There are various methods for this in Italy, the most common being to rinse the fresh olives in water, then boil them in a salt solution. They are left in the salt solution after they cool, kept there for a month, then the entire process is repeated. It takes another month for them to lose their bitter taste. After this time they are ready to eat. They are sometimes marinated in olive oil with herbs, garlic, peppers or spices to make them even tastier. The process is more or less the same for green as for black olives.

Green or black

The colour of an olive says nothing about the variety, only about ripeness.

As olives ripen on the tree, they change in colour from green to purple and eventually black.

Capers

Capers are small flower buds of the caper bush. Look carefully and you can see the little petals. They come in various shapes and sizes, the largest often being the sharpest and the smallest the most delicate-tasting. They are picked by hand, then packed in salt or vinegar – or both, as you often find them. Many Italians believe that capers lose their flavour when packed in vinegar. It is definitely worth the trouble to go out and find proper Italian capers in salt. Both the taste and texture are quite different from the vinegar variety. Soak them for a bit in cold water, then drain. This will allow their unique flavour to unfold.

Caper berries

Caper berries are the fruit of the caper bush. They are larger than the flower buds and sold with their stems still attached.

If you ever get the chance, pay attention to Italian women when they make their own tortellini, chatting amicably as they shape the little parcels in a flash. You will learn that making your own pasta is something the fingers learn to do on their own after a whole lot of tortellini-making. Try it out yourself; after you've done it once, it certainly gets faster. But don't ever hope to win a race against those Italian women! Filled pasta, just like *any other kind, comes in many different shapes.* Ravioli are squares, while agnolotti are half-moons, pansotti triangles and fagottini 'little envelopes'. *Tortellini are half-moons* with the points folded inward, cappellacci *triangles folded the same way,* looking something like a bishop's hat. They are great as a starter for special occasions and will be sure to impress anyone with the attention to detail that goes into them.

Filled pasta

The ideal dish for a large group of people is lasagne or another filled pasta, because these can be made in advance, then baked to serve.

Fresh ravioli can be kept in the refrigerator for up to two days if well-sealed. It can also be frozen (given that the filling will allow it). First place the ravioli in a tray in the freezer, taking care not to let the individual ravioli touch (they will freeze together otherwise). Once frozen through, simply place them in a plastic container or freezer bag. Keep them in the freezer until the moment you want to use them, then throw them straight into (a whole lot of) boiling water; use two pots if necessary. The cooking time is not much longer than when fresh, so test one after a bit to see how they're doing.

All of the following recipes make four servings.

Caramella with smoked salmon and lemon cream sauce

For the pasta dough:
300g (10.5oz) Italian pasta flour (type '00'), sifted
3 eggs
half tsp. salt

For the filling:
100g (3.5oz) smoked salmon flakes
100g (3.5oz) fresh salmon, diced
200g (7oz) ricotta
juice and zest of 1 lemon
small handful of fresh chives, minced
125 ml (0.5 cup) crème fraîche
salt and pepper

1. Put the flour in a pile and make a pit in the middle. Break the eggs into the pit and add the salt. Using a fork, carefully stir from the middle outward until all the flour is mixed with the egg. Knead for 10-15 minutes or until the dough is soft and elastic. Cover in plastic wrap and let it rest for at least 30 minutes to set.
2. For the filling, combine the salmon flakes, fresh salmon, ricotta, 1 tbsp lemon zest and half of the chives.
3. Roll the pasta dough out and slice it into rectangles measuring approx. 8x5cm. Place a spoonful of filling on each rectangle and roll the dough up lengthwise. Pinch the ends together well and twist them slightly, as if wrapping a toffee.
4. Boil the caramella for approx. 5 minutes in a large pot of salted water.
5. For the sauce, combine the crème fraîche, lemon juice and the rest of the chives. Add salt and pepper to taste.
6. Strain the caramella well. When dry, portion on to plates and serve the sauce on the side.

Tortellini with veal and parmesan

For the pasta dough:
300g (10.5oz) Italian pasta flour (type '00'), sifted
3 eggs
half tsp. salt

For the filling:
100g (3.5oz) veal, minced
small handful of mixed fresh herbs (such as parsley, tarragon and basil), minced
1 egg, beaten
salt and pepper
approx. 100g (3.5oz) Parmesan cheese, grated

1. Put the flour in a pile and make a pit in the middle. Break the eggs into the pit and add the salt. Using a fork, carefully stir from the middle outward until all the flour is mixed with the egg. Knead for 10-15 minutes or until the dough is soft and elastic. Cover in plastic wrap and let it rest for at least 30 minutes to set.
2. For the filling, combine the meat, egg, fresh herbs and some salt and pepper. Add just enough Parmesan to make the filling good and stiff.
3. On a dry, floured surface, roll the dough out to rectangular sheets less than 1 cm thick. Using a round ridged mould or cookie cutter, cut small rounds out of the sheet. Place a spoonful of filling on each round and dampen the edges slightly. Fold the rounds double and gently pinch the ends together. Fold the points towards each other, pressing them together firmly so they won't come undone.
4. Boil the tortellini 3 to 4 minutes in a large pot of boiling salted water.
5. Divide the tortellini over 4 plates and sprinkle with the rest of the Parmesan cheese. Serve immediately.

The colour of an egg yolk can vary enormously. This is not a reflection of the chicken's living conditions, but its diet. If the chicken is raised mostly on grain, the yolk will remain light in colour. If the bird gets a lot of carotene-rich foods, then it will produce eggs with darker yolks.

ⓥ Ravioli with peppers, ricotta, aubergine and mascarpone

1 sweet red pepper, diced

4 tbsp olive oil

1 aubergine, 1/3 cut into small cubes, the rest sliced into half-circles.

100g (3.5oz) ricotta

50g (1.75oz) mascarpone

salt and pepper

6 cloves of garlic, thinly sliced

12 basil leaves, cut into thin strips

2 tbsp black olives, pitted and halved

2 tbsp balsamic vinegar

For the pasta dough:

300g (10.5oz) Italian pasta flour (type '00'), sifted

3 eggs

half tsp. Salt

1. Put the flour in a pile on a clean surface and make a pit in the middle. Break the eggs into the pit and add the salt. Using a fork, carefully stir from the middle outward until all the flour is mixed with the eggs. Knead for 10-15 minutes or until the dough is soft and elastic. Cover in plastic wrap and let sit for at least 30 minutes to set.

2. For the filling, sauté half the diced pepper together with the aubergine cubes in 1 tbsp of olive oil for several minutes. Add the ricotta and mascarpone, stir well and add salt and pepper to taste.

3. On a dry, floured surface, roll the dough out to rectangular sheets less than 1cm thick. Imagine a line running down the middle of each sheet. Place spoonfuls of filling on one side of this line. Moisten the dough around each spoonful of filling with a wet brush. Fold each sheet double and carefully press the dough together so it is closed around the filling. Cut out the individual ravioli with a pastry wheel or sharp knife and seal the edges with the prongs of a fork.

4. Sauté the garlic in the olive oil until golden brown, then add the aubergine slices. Cook another 2 minutes or so, then add the remaining diced pepper and cook 1 minute more. Turn off the heat and stir in the basil.

5. Boil the ravioli for approx. 3 minutes in a large pot of boiling salted water.

6. Portion the aubergine and sweet pepper sauté on to plates and top with the ravioli. Garnish with olives and a drizzle of balsamic vinegar. Serve immediately.

The aubergine originally comes from Asia and belongs to the same family as the tomato. In the west, most people are only familiar with the large purple variety, though there are also aubergines the exact size and colour of chicken eggs – hence the term 'eggplant'. There are also pink, yellow, green and spotted varieties. Mini-aubergines, not much larger than a marble, are used quite heavily in Thai cuisine.

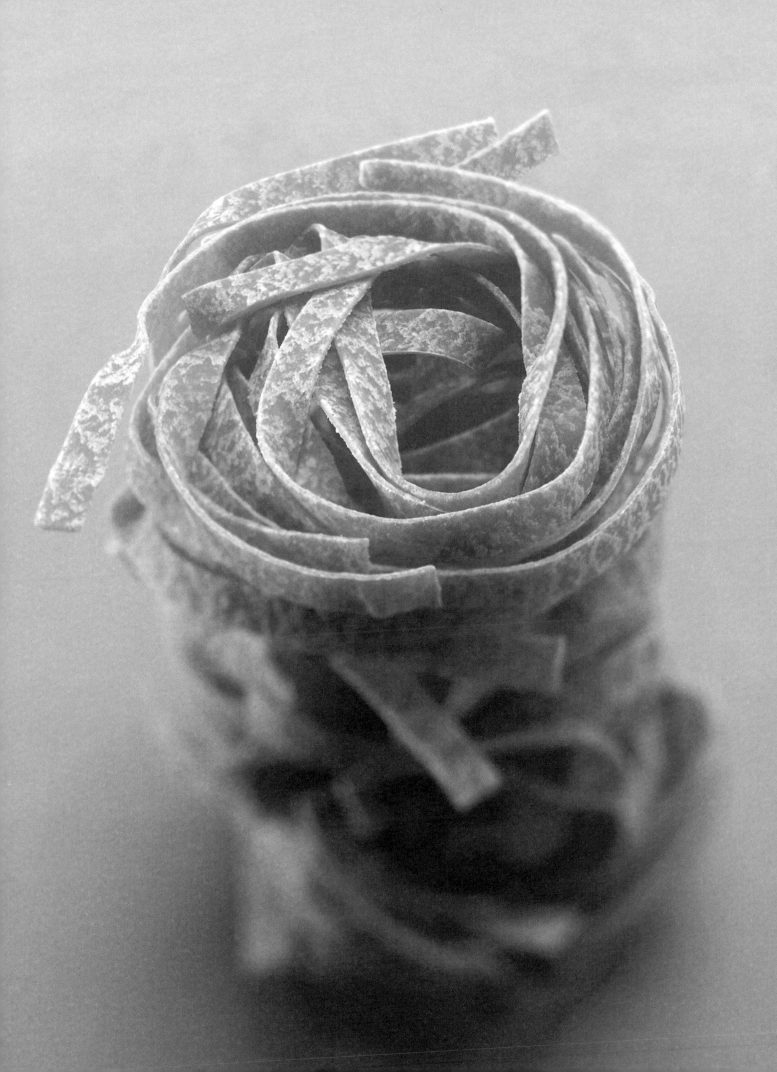

ⓥRavioli with artichoke mousse and tomato sauce

For the pasta dough:

300g (10.5oz) Italian pasta flour (type '00'), sifted

3 eggs

half tsp. salt

For the filling:

1 can of artichoke hearts in oil (400g)

1 clove of garlic, pressed

small handful of basil leaves, chopped

50g (1.75oz) Parmesan cheese, grated

salt and pepper

For the tomato sauce:

3 tbsp olive oil

1 carrot, thinly sliced

1 onion, thinly sliced

1 celery stalk, thinly sliced

400g (14oz) tomatoes, fresh (peeled) or peeled Italian tomatoes in the tin, coarsely chopped

2 tbsp fresh herbs (such as basil, oregano, parsley and thyme) plus extra basil strips for garnish

salt and pepper

1. For the tomato sauce, heat the oil in a pan and sauté the carrot, onion and celery. Add the tomatoes and fresh herbs, reduce the heat and simmer gently for 20 minutes. Taste, adding salt and pepper if necessary.

2. Put the flour in a pile on a clean surface and make a pit in the middle. Break the eggs into the pit and add the salt. Using a fork, carefully stir from the middle outward until all the flour is mixed with the eggs. Knead for 10-15 minutes or until the dough is soft and elastic. Cover in plastic wrap and let it rest for at least 30 minutes to set.

3. For the filling, puree the artichoke hearts, garlic, basil and Parmesan cheese with an hand-held blender until you have a smooth mousse. Pour in a little of the oil from the artichoke jar for a creamier texture. Add salt and pepper to taste.

4. On a dry, floured surface, roll the dough out to rectangular sheets less than 1 cm thick. Imagine a line running down the middle of each sheet. Place spoonfuls of filling on one side of this line. Moisten the dough around each spoonful of filling with a wet brush. Fold each sheet double and carefully press the dough together so it is closed around the filling. Using a (ridged) ravioli cutter, cut half-moons (agnolotti) out of the dough. Make sure that the edges are firmly sealed together.

5. Cook the agnolotti 3 to 4 minutes in a large pot of boiling salted water.

6. Divide the agnolotti and the tomato sauce over 4 plates and garnish with the basil. Serve immediately.

Agnolotti is a kind of ravioli made from small rounds of pasta dough. It has its origins in Piedmont, where pasta was stuffed with a combination of vegetables and meat remnants.

ⓥ Tortellini ricotta e spinazi with mushroom sauce

200ml (7oz) vegetable stock
100ml (3.5oz) sherry
100ml (3.5oz) single cream
300g (10.5oz) button mushrooms (1/3 finely chopped and 2/3 sliced)
400g (14 oz) ricotta and spinach tortellini (Grand'Italia)

1. Pour the stock, sherry and cream into a saucepan and stir in the chopped mushrooms.
2. Bring to a boil, then simmer for another 10 minutes or until the liquid is reduced by half. Strain the sauce.
3. Meanwhile, cook the tortellini in a large pot of boiling salted water.
4. Reheat the sauce and stir in the mushroom slices. Simmer for 1 minute.
5. Serve the tortellini and sauce on deep plates and top with freshly ground pepper.

ⓥ Tortellini tricolore with sweet pepper sauce

200ml (7oz) vegetable stock
100ml (3.5oz) dry white wine
1 tbsp tomato puree
1 sweet red pepper, diced
1 sweet green pepper, diced
1 sweet yellow pepper, diced
400g (14oz) tortellini tricolore (Grand'Italia)

1. Heat the stock and white wine, then stir in the tomato puree and keep on low heat for 4 minutes.
2. Add the diced peppers and simmer gently for another 4 minutes.
3. Cook the tortellini in a large pot of boiling salted water.
4. Strain well and portion the pasta into bowls. Top with the sauce. Serve immediately.

Conchiglioni with ricotta, green peas and béchamel

1 tbsp butter
1 shallot, minced
1 tbsp flour
200ml (7oz) milk
100g (3.5oz) Parmesan cheese, grated
200g (7oz) green peas
450g (1lb) ricotta
400g (14oz) conchiglioni (large pasta shells)

1. Preheat the oven to 200°C (400°F or gas mark 6).
2. For the béchamel sauce: melt the butter in a small saucepan. Sauté the shallot until it softens, then add the flour and cook another minute (do not allow to brown). Gradually whisk the milk into the butter mixture. Turn the heat to low and gently simmer the sauce for a minute or two. Stir in 50 grams of cheese.
3. Cook the peas for approx. 2 minutes in boiling salted water until tender.
4. Combine the ricotta with the rest of the cheese and stir in the peas.
5. Cook the pasta shells until al dente in a large pot of boiling salted water. Remove from the water and place on a tea towel to drain.
6. Stuff the shells with the ricotta mixture and place them in a greased casserole dish. Spoon a little of the béchamel sauce into each one.
7. Bake for approx. 10 minutes or until well cooked.

Ⓥ Cannelloni with purslane, ricotta and tomato sauce

500g (18oz) purslane
4 tomatoes, seeded and diced
small handful of basil leaves, chopped
200g (7oz) ricotta
salt and freshly ground pepper
butter for greasing
250g (9oz) cannelloni (precooked if necessary: read the
instructions on the package)
50g (1.75oz) Parmesan cheese, coarsely grated

For the tomato sauce:

400g (14oz) tomatoes (fresh or peeled Italian tomatoes in
the tin)
3 tbsp olive oil
1 carrot, finely chopped
1 onion, minced
1 celery stalk, finely chopped
2 cloves of garlic, peeled
1 red chilli pepper, seeded and minced
2 tbsp fresh herbs (basil, parsley, oregano, thyme)

1. Preheat the oven to 200°C (400°F or gas mark 6).
2. For the tomato sauce, peel and coarsely chop the fresh tomatoes. If using tinned tomatoes, cut them into chunks and strain.
3. Heat the olive oil in a pan. Sauté the carrot, onion and celery until the onion is translucent, then add the garlic and chilli pepper. Stir in the tomatoes and herbs and add salt and pepper to taste. Simmer gently until the vegetables cook down to a thick sauce.
4. Meanwhile, bring a large pot of water to a boil. Add the rinsed purslane. As soon as it boils down, remove and transfer to a sieve to strain. Press as much liquid as you can out of the purslane.
5. Slice it thinly and place it in a mixing bowl. Mix in the diced tomato, the basil and ricotta and add salt and pepper to taste.
6. Stuff the canneloni with the purslane mixture (the easiest way to do this is with a pastry bag) and place them in a greased casserole dish. Cover with the tomato sauce and bake for 30 minutes in the preheated oven.
7. Remove from the oven and portion onto 4 plates. Sprinkle with Parmesan and serve immediately.

Purslane contains more omega-3 than any other leafy green vegetable. In many countries, the plant is not eaten as a vegetable, but used purely for medicinal purposes. It is said to lower your heart rate and relieve heartburn. The Greeks used it as a cure for constipation and inflammation of the urinary tract. And in Classical times, Plinius the Elder advised that it be worn as an amulet to keep demons away.

Tortellini formaggio

half tbsp olive oil

1 clove of garlic, minced

500g (18oz) tomatoes, quartered

200ml (7oz) vegetable stock

1 sprig of thyme

small handful of fresh basil

small handful of fresh parsley

salt and pepper

400g (14oz) tortellini ai formaggio (Grand'Italia)

100g (3.5oz) Parmesan cheese, grated

1. Heat the oil in a pan and sauté the garlic and tomatoes for 1 minute.
2. Pour in the stock and bring to a boil.
3. Turn the heat to low, place the fresh herbs on top and simmer for 15 minutes.
4. Remove the herbs (their flavour should be completely infused by now). Puree the sauce with an hand-held blender and add salt and pepper to taste.
5. Cook the tortellini until al dente in a large pot of boiling salted water. Strain and toss with the sauce.
6. Sprinkle with the cheese and serve immediately.

ⓥ Open lasagne with tomato, pesto and goat's cheese

8 lasagne sheets
olive oil for greasing
400g (14oz) soft goat's cheese
4 tomatoes, sliced
4 tbsp pesto (see basic recipe, page 82)

1. Preheat the oven to 200°C (400°F or gas mark 6).
2. Cook the lasagne sheets until al dente in a large pot of boiling salted water, following the directions on the package.
3. Using a cookie cutter, cut 16 rounds out of the lasagne sheets.
4. Grease a casserole dish with olive oil and set up four pasta 'towers' in it: for each, place a round of pasta on the bottom, cover with crumbled goat's cheese, a tomato slice, another pasta round and half a tablespoon of pesto. Continue layering in this order, ending with a pasta round. Coat the top with a little olive oil.
5. Bake for approx. 5 minutes or until the cheese just begins to melt. Serve immediately.

Delicious with a green salad.

ⓥ Cannelloni with spinach and aged cheese

500g (18oz) spinach, rinsed and chopped
small handful of basil leaves, chopped
250g (9oz) hard cheese, grated (set aside ¼ of this for sprinkling over top)
salt and freshly ground pepper
butter for greasing
250g (9oz) cannelloni
2 tbsp pine nuts

1. Preheat the oven to 200°C (400°F or gas mark 6).
2. Bring a large pot of water to a boil. Drop in the rinsed spinach. As soon as the spinach boils down, remove it and place in a sieve to drain. Press as much liquid as possible out of the spinach.
3. Mix the basil and a little more than half of the cheese into the spinach and add salt and pepper to taste.
4. Grease a casserole dish with butter. Stuff the cannelloni with the spinach mixture (this is easiest with a pastry bag) and place in the casserole dish. Sprinkle with the rest of the grated cheese and top with the pine nuts.
5. Bake for approx. 30 minutes or until golden brown and cooked through.

Basil is a symbol of love in Italy. In France it's called 'the royal herb' but has a lot of negative symbolism in Greece. Then again, according to African legend, it will protect you from scorpions. Whatever you believe, one thing is universally true: it should be used as freshly as possible.

Add basil to hot foods at the very last minute. It will quickly lose its flavour when exposed to too much heat. Never use dried basil; this has almost no discernible flavour and what little there is, is more reminiscent of hay than of this most aromatic herb.

Ravioli with hazelnut mascarpone sauce

150g (5oz) hazelnuts
200ml (7oz) vegetable broth
200g (7oz) mascarpone
400g (14oz) ravioli mezzaluna ai funghi porcini (Grand'Italia)
handful of rocket, chopped

1. Finely grind the hazelnuts in a food processor. Whisk the vegetable broth and mascarpone together until smooth. Stir in the nuts and simmer for five minutes on low heat. Puree with a hand-held blender until all the ingredients are well blended.

2. Cook the ravioli until al dente in a large pot of boiling salted water. Strain and portion on to plates.

3. Ladle some of the sauce over the ravioli and top with the rocket. Serve immediately.

Chilli peppers & spices

Amatriciana is not the same without them: fiery red chilli peppers! Pepper and other spices are usually used with moderation in most Italian dishes. Take away these unique seasonings, though, and Italian cuisine just would not have the same flair.

Peperoncini

When you think about Italian food, the first thing to come to mind may not be its spiciness. Southern Italians, though, can whip up some pretty lively dishes. The inhabitants of Basilicata, for instance, are known for growing their own chilli peppers – and not just for decoration either! Their pasta sauces and ragùs can be surprisingly hot. The smallest peperoncini are also the spiciest, earning the name of *diavolicci* (little devils). These are home-grown and home-dried as well, hanging in the sun along the walls of people's houses. The native dishes of Apulia are also heavily seasoned with chillis, including the famous orecchiette with broccoli and anchovy. The same goes for the recipes concocted by the shepherds of Abruzzi, such as spaghetti all'Amatriciana, with bacon and dried chillis.

Pepper

When an Italian recipe calls for pepper, it almost always refers to black peppercorns freshly ground in a pepper mill. Sometimes it goes into the pasta dough itself, adding pretty little black flecks and an extra bite.

Noce moscata

In Italy, nutmeg is freshly grated as a seasoning for a variety of foods, such as meat or pumpkin filling for ravioli, or added to béchamel sauce. Many ragùs are also rounded off with a little grated nutmeg.

Zafferano

Saffron is the most expensive spice by weight in the world. These tiny strands lend the brilliant yellow colour and delicate flavour to dishes like spaghetti allo zafferano with its silky smooth saffron cream sauce, and the Sicilian malloreddus, a type of golden yellow gnocchi. Saffron is nothing more than the stigmas of a special crocus, widely cultivated in the Abruzzo region and nicknamed, for good reason, 'the gold of Abruzzo'. Soak the strands for ten minutes in warm water before adding to a dish. A little goes a long way.

Giodo di garofano

Cloves are used quite sparingly in Italian cuisine. Sicilian cuscusu (a fish and couscous dish) is often made with cloves and bay. Fresh basil often has a slight clove flavour and aroma, especially if grown in an area which gets a lot of sun. A small pinch of ground clove is sometimes added to fresh pesto if the basil itself is not as aromatic as it should be.

...E FVERVNT · TERTIVM · ...
...VNIVERSVS · APPELLAVIT · ME · PATREM · PATRI...
... VLIA · ET · IN · FORO · AVG · SVB · QVADRIGIS · QVA...
...AGEBAM · SEPTVAGENSVMVM · SEXTVM
...MANAE · VEL · DIMISSIS · MILITIBVS · DENARI...
...ONANTIS · ET · FERETRI · APOLLINIS · DIV...
...RVM · DEVM · PENATIVM · IVVENTATIS...
...HALCIDICO · FORVM · AVGVSTVM · BA...
...THEATRVM · POMPEI · AQVARVM · R...
...A · ET · MVNERA · GLADIATORVM ·
...COLONIS · IN · ITALIA · OPPIDIS
...M · AMICIS · SENATORIBVSQVE

M·SEX... QVI... MA
IVLI·QVI... RIS·MA
MATRIS·MA
...ILICAM·IVL... IVL
...EFECI·CAP
...VOS·VIAM·
...ATQVE·ATH
...IN·PROVI
...QVORVM·

Index

A

Aged cheese

    Cannelloni with spinach and ~ — 274

    Three-cheese lasagne — 210

    Penne with ~ and avocado — 236

Agnolotti

    Ravioli with artichoke mousse and tomato sauce — 262

Anelletti

    Seafood stock with ~ — 124

Anchovies

    Tinned ~ — 178

    Bucatini con le sarde — 74

    Penne with fresh tuna and peppers — 192

    Crisp-fried spaghetti with anchovies and bread crumbs — 202

    Penne rigate with ~ and broccoli — 194

    Penne salad with tuna tapenade — 248

    Spaghetti alla puttanesca — 106

Artichokes

    Ravioli with artichoke mousse and tomato sauce — 262

    Tagliatelle with artichoke hearts and capers — 142

Asparagus

    Mezzi rigatoni with chicken and ~ — 244

    Pappardelle with asparagus carbonara — 212

Aubergine

    Macaroni with ~ and mozzarella — 152

    Ravioli with peppers, ricotta, ~ and mascarpone — 258

Avocado

    Penne with aged cheese and ~ — 236

B

Balsamic vinegar — 232

Balsamic dressing

    Mezzi rigatoni with chicken and asparagus — 244

Beans

    Orecchiette with ~ and raisins — 248

Béchamel sauce

    Conchiglioni with ricotta, green peas and ~ — 266

    Lasagne al forno — 92

    Lasagne with mozzarella and béchamel — 210

    Mushroom lasagne — 146

Beef bouillon with spaghettini and meatballs — 114

Beef, minced

    Lasagne al forno — 92

    Beef bouillon with spaghettini and meatballs — 114

    Tagliatelle alla Bolognese — 68

Beef, stewed

    Pipe rigate with ~ and San Daniele — 162

Bolognese

    Tagliatelle alla ~ — 40

Bottarga — 200

Bouillon

    ~ with green peas and pancetta — 118

    Minestrone — 102

    Minestrone with porcini mushrooms and chicken filet — 124

    Beef bouillon with spaghettini and meatballs — 114

    Tortellini in brodo rosso — 120

    Seafood stock with anelletti — 124

Bresaola

    Fusilli bucati with ~ and rucola — 238

Broccoli

    Penne Rigate with anchovies and ~ — 194

Bucatini

    ~ all'Amatriciana — 94

    ~ con le sarde — 74

C

Cannelloni

    ~ with purslane, ricotta and tomato sauce — 270

    ~ with spinach and aged cheese — 274

Capelli d'angelo

    Chicken soup with ~ — 128

Capers

    Olives & ~ — 252

    Tagliatelle with artichoke hearts and ~ — 142

Caramella with smoked salmon and lemon cream sauce — 256

Cashews

    Pipe rigate with ricotta nut sauce — 228

Cheese — 204

Fontina

Grana

Gorgonzola

Mascarpone

Mozzarella

Parmigiano-Reggiano

Pecorino

Ricotta

Ricotta salata

Cherry tomatoes

    Lasagnette with pomodorini 136

    Ricotta gnocchi 218

    Mezzi rigatoni with chicken and asparagus 244

Chicken

    Green tagliatelle with chicken fillet in white wine sauce 160

    Maccheroncini with chicken filet in mushroom sauce 166

    Mezzi rigatoni with ~ and asparagus 244

    Minestrone with porcini mushrooms and chicken filet 124

Chicken liver

    Tagliatelle alla Bolognese 40

Chicken soup with capelli d'angelo 128

Chilli peppers & spices 278

    Giodo di garofano

    Noce moscata

    Pepper

    Peperoncini

    Zafferano

Conchiglie

    ~ all'uovo with shrimp in creamy dill sauce 192

    Mushroom soup with ~ rigate 130

Conchiglioni with ricotta, green peas and béchamel sauce 266

Coquilles Saint-Jacques

    Cravattine with ~ 186

Courgette

    Fusilli tricolore with ~ flowers and sun-dried tomato sauce 138

    Green tagliatelle with chicken fillet in white wine sauce 160

    Tagliatelle with spring vegetables 154

Crab

    Fazzoletti with ~ in butter sauce 188

    Fusilli with salmon and seafood 246

    Gnocchi salad with fresh ~ and rucola 244

Cravattine with coquilles Saint-Jacques 186

Crisp-fried spaghetti with anchovies and bread crumbs 202

D

Dill

    Conchiglie all'uovo with shrimp in creamy dill sauce 192

E

Egg pasta

    Basic pasta dough recipe 37

    Caramella with smoked salmon and lemon cream sauce 256

    Conchiglie all'uovo with shrimp in creamy dill sauce 192

    Cravattine with coquilles Saint-Jacques 186

    Fazzoletti with crab in butter sauce 188

    Green tagliatelle with chicken fillet in white wine sauce 160

    Pappardelle with asparagus carbonara 212

    Ravioli di magro 90

    Ravioli with artichoke mousse and tomato sauce 262

    Ravioli with sweet peppers, ricotta, aubergine and mascarpone 258

    Stringhetti with saffron 208

    Tagliatelle alla Bolognese 68

    Tagliatelle all'uovo with gorgonzola and sage 216

    Tortellini with veal and parmesan 256

Eggplant: see Aubergine

F

Farfalle

    ~ alla boscaiola 78

    ~ with green sauce 152

Fazzoletti with crab in butter sauce 188

Fennel

    Bucatini con le sarde 74

Fettuccine

    ~ all'Alfredo 100

    ~ with spinach and fontina 230

Fettucelle with pork tenderloin in creamy mushroom sauce 172

Fontina

    Fettuccine with spinach and ~ 230

Fresh tomato soup with orecchiette 116

Fusilli

    ~ bucati with bresaola and rucola 238

~ with fresh salmon, watercress and horseradish 196

~ with minced lamb and mustard 174

~ with salmon and seafood 246

~ tricolore with courgette flowers 138

G

Garlic 214

    Ravioli with sweet peppers, ricotta, aubergine and mascarpone 258

    Spaghetti alle vongole 84

    Spaghetti con aglio e olio 98

    Spaghetti met bottarga 200

    Whole-grain penne with sausage and roasted ~ 170

Glasswort

    Tagliatelle with seabass and ~ 184

Goat's cheese

    Three-cheese lasagne 210

    Open lasagne with tomato, pesto and ~ 274

    Whole-grain spaghetti with roasted peppers and ~ 224

Filled pasta 30

Gnocchi 44

    ~ alla Romana 88

    Gnocchi salad with fresh crab and rucola 244

    Ricotta gnocchi 218

Golden rules 19

Gorgonzola 232

    Farfalle alla boscaiola 78

Green beans: see Haricots verts

Green tagliatelle with chicken fillet in white wine sauce 160

H

Ham

    Pappardelle with asparagus carbonara 212

Hare

    Pappardelle alla lepre 80

Haricots verts

    Farfalle with green sauce 152

    Trenette alla Genovese 82

Hazelnuts

    Ravioli with hazelnut mascarpone sauce 276

Herbs 132

    Basil (basilico)

    Bay (alloro)

    Oregano (origano)

    Parsley (prezzemolo)

    Rosemary (rosmarino)

    Rocket (rucola)

    Sage (salvia)

Herb oil

    Tagliatelle with seabass and glasswort 184

Horseradish

    Fusilli with fresh salmon, watercress and ~ 196

I

Italian meats & dried sausage 156

    Parma ham

    San Daniele

    Bresaola

    Pancetta

    Lardo and speck

    Salami

J

Jacob's shells: see Coquilles Saint-Jacques

Jus

    Whole-grain penne with sausage and roasted garlic 170

L

Lamb, minced

    Fusilli with ~ and mustard 174

Lemon cream sauce

    Caramella with smoked salmon and ~ 256

Long pasta (pasta lunga) 26, 27

    Tagliatelle all'uovo with ~ and sage 216

    Penne with pear, pistachio and ~ 228

Lasagne

    ~ al forno 92

    ~ with mozzarella and béchamel 210

    Mushroom ~ 146

    Open ~ with tomato, pesto and goat's cheese 274

    Pappardelle and ~

    Three-cheese ~ 210

Lasagnette
    ~ with pomodorini and garlic — 136
    ~ with salmon and crème fraîche chive sauce — 196
Linguine
    ~ with salami — 176
    ~ with scampi and garlic mustard sauce — 182
    Black ~ with pulpo salad — 242

M

Mafaldine with salame cacciatore — 166
Macaroni with aubergine and mozzarella — 152
Maccheroncini
    ~ with chicken filet in mushroom sauce — 166
    ~ with pancetta and mascarpone — 222
Mascarpone
    Farfalle alla boscaiola — 78
    Maccheroncini with pancetta and ~ — 222
    Ravioli with hazelnut mascarpone sauce — 276
    Ravioli with sweet peppers, ricotta, aubergine and ~ — 258
Marinade
    Papperdelle alla lepre — 80
Meatballs
    Beef bouillon with spaghettini and ~ — 114
Meat broth: see Jus
Mezzi rigatoni
    ~ with chicken and asparagus — 244
    ~ with snow peas and tuna — 236
Minestrone — 102
    ~ with porcini mushrooms and chicken filet — 124
Mustard
    Fusilli with minced lamb and ~ — 174
    Linguine with scampi and garlic mustard sauce — 182
Mozzarella
    Lasagne with ~ and béchamel — 210
    Macaroni with aubergine and ~ — 152
Mushroom
    ~ lasagne — 146
    ~ soup with conchiglie rigate — 130
    Farfalle alla boscaiola — 78
    Fettucelle with pork tenderloin in creamy mushroom sauce — 172
    Maccheroncini with chicken filet in mushroom sauce — 166

Tagliatelle with spring vegetables — 154
Tortellini ricotta e spinaci with mushroom sauce — 264

O

Octopus
    Black linguine with pulpo salad — 242
    Fusilli with salmon and seafood — 246
Olive oil — 96
Olives
    Fusilli with salmon and seafood — 246
    ~ & capers — 252
    Penne salad with tuna tapenade — 248
    Spaghetti alla marinara — 108
    Spaghetti alla puttanesca — 106
    Spaghetti with olives, tomatoes and rocket — 140
    Tortiglioni with spinach and olive tapenade — 184
Open lasagne with tomato, pesto and goat's cheese — 274
Orecchiette
    ~ with beans and raisins — 248
    Fresh tomato soup with ~ — 116
Oyster mushrooms
    Mushroom lasagne — 146

P

Paglia e fieno with pesto rosso — 150
Pancetta
    Stock with green peas and ~ — 118
    Bucatini all'Amatriciana — 94
    Maccheroncini with ~ and mascarpone — 222
Pappardelle
    ~ alla lepre — 80
    ~ with asparagus carbonara — 212
    ~ with sun-dried tomatoes and pine nuts — 148
Parma ham
    Pipe rigate with ~ and green peas — 176
Parmesan cheese
    Three-cheese lasagne — 210
    Tortellini formaggio — 272
    Tortellini with veal and parmesan — 256
    Tortiglioni with tomato and parmesan — 216
Pears
    Penne with ~, pistachios and gorgonzola — 228

Peas, green
    Stock with ~ and pancetta ... 118
    Conchiglioni with ricotta, ~ and béchamel sauce ... 266
    Pipe rigate with parma ham and ~ ... 176
Pecorino
    Pipe rigate with walnut pecorino sauce ... 222
Penne
    ~ alla carbonara ... 70
    ~ with sausage and roasted garlic ... 170
    ~ with aged cheese and avocado ... 236
    ~ with pear, pistachios and gorgonzola ... 228
    ~ with fresh tuna and peppers ... 192
    ~ rigate with anchovies and broccoli ... 194
Penne salad with tuna tapenade ... 248
Penne alla carbonara ... 70
    Tagliatelle alla Bolognese ... 68
Peppers, sweet
    Penne with fresh tuna and ~ ... 192
    Ravioli with ~, ricotta, aubergine and mascarpone ... 258
    Tortellini tricolore with sweet pepper sauce ... 264
    Whole-grain spaghetti with roasted ~ and goat's cheese ... 224
Perciatelli with spicy tomato sauce ... 148
Pesto
    Cabbage soup with ~ ... 126
    Open lasagne with tomato, ~ and goat's cheese ... 274
    Paglia e fieno with ~ rosso ... 150
    ~ alla Genovese ... 110
    Trenette alla Genovese ... 82
Pine nuts
    Paglia e fieno with pesto rosso ... 150
    Pappardelle with sun-dried tomatoes and pine nuts ... 148
Pipe rigate
    Roasted vegetable soup with ~ ... 128
    ~ with parma ham and green peas ... 176
    ~ with ricotta nut sauce ... 228
    ~ with stewed beef and San Daniele ... 162
    ~ with walnut pecorino sauce ... 222
Pistachios
    Penne with pear, ~ and gorgonzola ... 228
Pomodori ... 220
Porcini mushrooms
    Farfalle alla boscaiola ... 78

Minestrone with ~ and chicken filet ... 124
Pork tenderloin
    Fettucelle with ~ in creamy mushroom sauce ... 172
Potatoes
    Cabbage soup with pesto ... 126
    Minestrone ... 102
    Trenette alla Genovese ... 82
Prosciutto crudo
    Tortelloni prosciutto crudo in creamy tomato sauce ... 164
Pulpo (fresh octopus)
    Black linguine with pulpo salad ... 242
Purslane
    Cannelloni with ~, ricotta and tomato sauce ... 270

R
Ragù ... 68, 80
Raisins
    Orecchiette with beans and ~ ... 248
Ravioli ... 38
    ~ di magro ... 90
    ~ with artichoke mousse and tomato sauce ... 262
    ~ with hazelnut mascarpone sauce ... 276
    ~ with sweet peppers, ricotta, aubergine and mascarpone ... 258
Red wine
    Tortellini in brodo rosso ... 120
    Pappardelle alla lepre ... 80
Ricotta
    Cannelloni with purslane, ~ and tomato sauce ... 270
    Conchiglioni with ~, green peas and béchamel sauce ... 266
    Pipe rigate with ricotta nut sauce ... 228
    Tortellini ~ e spinaci with mushroom sauce ... 264
    Ravioli di magro ... 90
    Ravioli with sweet peppers, ~, aubergine and mascarpone ... 258
    ~ gnocchi ... 218
Roasted vegetable soup with pipe rigate ... 128
Rocket
    Fusilli bucati with bresaola and ~ ... 238
    Gnocchi salad with fresh crab and ~ ... 244
    Spaghetti with olives, tomatoes and ~ ... 140

Ravioli with artichoke mousse and tomato sauce	262
Spaghetti alla marinara	108
Spaghetti alla Napoletana	70
Spaghetti with olives, tomatoes and rocket	140
Spaghetti with fresh tomato sauce	140
Tortiglioni with ~ and parmesan	216

S

Saffron	
Stringhetti with ~	208
Sage	
Tagliatelle all'uovo with gorgonzola and ~	216
Salads	
Gnocchi salad with fresh crab and rocket	244
Penne salad with tuna tapenade	248
Black linguine with pulpo salad	242
Salami	
Linguine with ~	176
Salmon	
Caramella with smoked ~ and lemon cream sauce	256
Fusilli with fresh ~, watercress and horseradish	196
Fusilli with ~ and seafood	246
Lasagnette with ~ and crème fraîche chive sauce	196
Samphire, marsh: see Glasswort	
San Daniele	
Pipe rigate with stewed beef and ~	162
Sardines	
Bucatini con le sarde	74
Sausage	
Whole-grain penne with ~ and roasted garlic	170
Scallops: see Coquilles Saint-Jacques	
Scampi	
Fusilli with salmon and seafood	246
Linguine with ~ and garlic mustard sauce	182
Seabass	
Tagliatelle with ~ and samphire	184
Seafood	
Fusilli with salmon and ~	246
~ stock with alfabetini	124
Black linguine with pulpo salad	242
Shiitakes	
Mushroom lasagne	146

Short pasta (pasta corta)	28, 29
Cabbage soup with pesto	126
Shrimp	
Conchiglie all'uovo with ~ in creamy dill sauce	192
Snow peas	
Farfalle with green sauce	152
Mezzi rigatoni with ~ and tuna	236
Tagliatelle with spring vegetables	154
Soups with pasta	112
Cabbage soup with pesto	126
Chicken soup with capelli d'angelo	128
Mushroom soup with conchiglie rigate	130
Roasted vegetable soup with pipe rigate	128
Vegetable soup with tortellini	118
Spinach soup with mini noodles	114
Fresh tomato soup with orecchiette	116
Spaghetti	
Crisp-fried ~ with anchovies and bread crumbs	202
~ alla marinara	108
~ alla Napoletana	70
~ alla puttanesca	106
~ alle vongole	84
~ con aglio e olio	98
~ with bottarga	200
~ with fresh tomato sauce	140
~ with olives, tomatoes and rocket	140
Whole-grain ~ with roasted peppers and goat's cheese	224
Spaghettini	
Beef bouillon with ~ and meatballs	114
Farfalle with green sauce	152
Trenette alla Genovese	82
Orecchiette with beans and raisins	248
Spinach	
Cannelloni with ~ and aged cheese	274
Fettuccine with ~ and fontina	230
Ravioli di magro	90
Spinach soup with mini noodles	114
Tortiglioni with ~ and olive tapenade	184
Tortellini ricotta e spinaci with mushroom sauce	264
Spring cabbage	
Cabbage soup with pesto	126
Tagliatelle with tenderloin and truffle sauce	162

Stock: see Bouillon

Stringhetti with saffron — 208

T

Tagliatelle 40

Green ~ with chicken fillet in white wine sauce — 160

~ alla Bolognese — 68

~ all'uovo with gorgonzola and sage — 216

~ with artichoke hearts and capers — 142

~ with tenderloin and truffle sauce — 162

~ with parsley lemon oil — 136

~ with spring vegetables — 154

~ with seabass and samphire — 184

Tapenade

Penne salad with tuna tapenade — 248

Tenderloin

Tagliatelle with ~ and truffle sauce — 162

Tomato (pomodori) — 220

Bucatini all'Amatriciana — 94

Cannelloni with purslane, ricotta and tomato sauce — 270

Lasagnette with pomodorini and garlic — 136

Open lasagne with ~, pesto and goat's cheese — 274

Pappardelle alla lepre — 80

Pappardelle with sun-dried tomatoes and pine nuts — 148

Perciatelli with spicy tomato sauce — 148

Tomato sauce — 32

Tomato soup with orecchiette — 116

Tortellini — 39

Vegetable soup with ~ — 118

~ formaggio — 272

~ in brodo rosso — 120

~ with veal and parmesan — 256

~ ricotta e spinaci with mushroom sauce — 264

~ tricolore with sweet pepper sauce — 264

Tortelloni prosciutto crudo in creamy tomato sauce — 164

Tortiglioni

~ with spinach and olive tapenade — 184

~ with tomato and parmesan — 216

Trenette

~ alla Genovese — 82

Truffle sauce

Tagliatelle with tenderloin and ~ — 162

Tuna

Mezzi rigatoni with snow peas and ~ — 236

Penne with fresh ~ and peppers — 192

Penne salad with tuna tapenade — 248

V

Veal

Tortellini with ~ and parmesan — 256

Vegetable soup

~ with pipe rigate — 128

~ with tortellini — 118

Venus clams

Spaghetti alle vongole — 84

W

Walnuts

Pipe rigate with walnut pecorino sauce — 222

Watercress

Fusilli with fresh salmon, ~ and horseradish — 196

White wine

Farfalle alla boscaiola — 78

Green tagliatelle with chicken fillet in white wine sauce — 160

Maccheroncini with chicken filet in mushroom sauce — 167

Spaghetti alle vongole — 84

Whole-grain spaghetti with roasted peppers and goat's cheese — 224

Z

Zucchini: see Courgette